When the River Ice Flows, I Will Come Home

When the River Ice Flows, I Will Come Home

A Memoir

Elisa
Brodinsky Miller

BOSTON
2020

Library of Congress Cataloging-in-Publication Data

Names: Brodinsky Miller, Elisa, author.
Title: When the river ice flows, I will come home : a memoir / Elisa
   Brodinsky Miller.
Description: Boston : Cherry Orchard Books, 2020. | Includes
   bibliographical references.
Identifiers: LCCN 2019046140 (print) | LCCN 2019046141 (ebook) |
   ISBN 9781644692790 (hardcover) | ISBN 9781644692806 (paperback) |
   ISBN 9781644692813 (adobe pdf)
Subjects: LCSH: Brodinsky Miller, Elisa—Family. | Jewish women—United
   States—Biography.
Classification: LCC E184.37.M545 A3 2020 (print) | LCC E184.37.M545
   (ebook) | DDC 929.20947—dc23
LC record available at https://lccn.loc.gov/2019046140
LC ebook record available at https://lccn.loc.gov/2019046141

Grateful acknowledgment is made to Tony Kushner for permission to reprint
an excerpt from Angels in America by Tony Kushner. Copyright © 1992, 1994,
1996, 2013 by Tony Kushner. Published by Theatre Communications Group.
Used by permission of Theatre Communications Group.

ISBN 978-1-644692-79-0 (hardback)
ISBN 978-1-644692-80-6 (paperback)
ISBN 978-1-644692-81-3 (adobe pdf)
ISBN 978-1-644693-53-7 (ePub)

Book design by Tatiana Vernikov
Cover design by Joe Menth

Published by Cherry Orchard Books (imprint of Academic Studies Press)
1577 Beacon Street
Brookline, MA 02446, USA
press@academicstudiespress. com
www.academicstudiespress. com

To

Rachael and **Amos**
Tillie and **Aditieh**

Though for no other cause, yet for this,
that posterity may know we have not loosely
through silence permitted things to pass away
as in a dream.

—Richard Hooker,
Of the Laws of Ecclesiastical Polity

CONTENTS

Foreword   8
1. A Cache of Letters   9
2. Gone to America   16
3. War Disrupts   24
4. Inflation Spirals   34
5. Scythe against Stone   43
6. Wrapping Tefillin   47
7. Eli Sends Money   52
8. Making Ends Meet   56
9. My Parents Separate, Reconcile, Divorce   61
10. Meer Joins the Red Army   66
11. My Marriage, My Divorce   76
12. Reindeer in the Arctic   80
13. Taiga, Tundra, Gulag   88
14. Papa, Come Home!   97
15. Jewish Passion, Jewish Suffering   101
16. A Terrible Night   104
17. It Is My Turn Now to Try   115
18. The Soul Suffers   118
19. Ragamuffins, Barefoot, and Hungry   123
20. When the River Ice Flows   134
21. Waiting to Leave   145
22. The *Moloch* of Ambition   152
23. In Riga, at Last   157
24. Olga   171
25. Al Anon   177
26. A Plot in the Jewish Section   180

Afterword   183
Acknowledgments   185
About the Author   186
Sources   187

Appendix I. My Father's Travel Notes   188
Appendix 2. Understanding the Russian Pale   196

Maps
   Southwestern (Ukrainian) Provinces of the Russian Empire, 1914   16
   Kiev Province and the Pale of Jewish Settlement within   17
      the Russian Empire, 1914
   Gulag Territory (Yakutiia)   81
   Working in the Tundra   92
   Siziman Bay Gulag Camp   96
   Civil War 1912-1921, with Railroad Lines   99
   After the Pogrom of 1920, Manya's Family Disperses   125
   Amur and Ussuri Rivers Ice Breakup   139
   Railroad Lines 1918   158
   Getting to the Ship at Liepeija, Latvia   170

FOREWORD

I do not know this woman. . . .
I do not know her and yet I know her.
She was . . . not a person but a whole kind of person,
the ones who crossed the ocean,
who brought with us to America
the villages of Russia and Lithuania . . . .

Descendants of this immigrant woman,
you do not grow up in America,
you and your children and their children
with the *goyische* names,
you do not live in America, no such place exists.
Your clay is the clay of Litvak shtetl,
your air the air of the steppes.

Because she carried the old world
on her back across the ocean, in a boat,
and put down on Grand Concourse Avenue, or in Flatbush,
and she worked that earth into your bones,
and you pass it to your children, this ancient,
ancient culture and home. . . .

You can never make that crossing that she made,
for such Great Voyages in this world do not any more exist.
But every day of your lives the miles that voyage
between that place and this one you cross.
Every day. You understand me?
In you that journey is.

—Tony Kushner,
selections from *Angels in America*

1. A Cache of Letters

By the rules of the retirement center in Bloomfield, Connecticut where my father had lived, the family was allotted five working days after his death to clear out the belongings from his cottage. My brother and I had agreed: we wouldn't save any furniture, just the china, the stemware, the samovar, and the contents of his study. It all was to go into a storage unit near his home in Wallingford, CT. Together, later, we three siblings would sort through it all. Each of us would take what we wanted and we'd toss the rest. We doubted there would be any scraps between us; we three are much too different. Exactly a year after our father's death, I traveled from Seattle, my sister came from Charlotte, to stay with my brother and his wife.

I knew the contents of many of those boxes marked "Books—from study." During my visits to my father I had often looked at his books, on occasion he would gift me one or two. It was torment to stand in the storage unit and watch both my brother and my sister tear through these. Nothing seemed to matter to them. Especially the books. Even before I got a chance to say I want it, my brother was ready to put a book in the toss pile. Books that meant a lot to my father and books I wanted to keep. Once, my brother who was trying to send an oversized book into the toss bin, misjudged and instead of the toss bin the book landed on the concrete floor flat open with its spine broken and pages awry. Like kicking someone down the stairs and watching them land sprawled out and hurt. Aggression. Like when the *pogromschiks* entered a synagogue to tear it apart and hurled all the sacred books to the sidewalk to be burnt.

Angry I was, and now nothing much left to do except to say I'll take all his books, his notes, papers and sort through them more leisurely later. "But Annie doesn't want any of this in her house. There might be silverfish in the books or in the papers," my sister Molly says. My sister who took the name of my grandmother, Manya. "You can't take all this there, Annie and Mike don't like clutter."

Silverfish notwithstanding, the whole shebang was now under my gaze in the basement of my brother's house. There were scores of postcards and letters. Amongst those letters was a small notebook wrapped in pink tissue paper. Written on the pink paper was the word "Ucraine." I opened this small notebook of 68 numbered pages written in Russian and noted the title page: Travel Notes. The pages were brittle but the Russian handwriting was clear enough. I read the first sentence of the entry, dated August 29, 1922. *We left Kiev at 12:00 noon.* I turned to the last page 68 and read the last entry. *We waited on the benches [of Ellis Island] until our names were called . . . .* My father, always the journalist, had left me the perfect gift. I'd have him all to myself for quite a while. I couldn't wait to take everything back to Seattle.

Finding so many letters and postcards as well as my father's travel diary in Russian intensified my delight in the art of translation. I knew I eventually would be able to master the various handwritings and gain meaning and context from what I read. Translation was a tool I used in my work: beginning with my dissertation research and also my subsequent writings about contemporary Russia.

Once back at home, I was disciplined and patient. I had just sold my business, a small company publishing commercial intelligence on the Russian Far East. I would have the time. This was going to be a big project and I would start carefully, methodically. The letters and postcards addressed to Eli Brodinsky, my grandfather, in Wilmington

Eli leaves his wife and six children, 1914.

Delaware, start just days after Eli's ship (the m/v Carminia) left Liverpool on May 23, 1914, and continued for eight years until the week when those he left behind—his wife and six children (but one)—boarded *their* ship on September 26, 1922 (the m/v Lithuania) to join him.

Eight Years.

Eight very long years.

I could read Russian. But I couldn't read Yiddish and the first letters to Eli were entirely in Yiddish. I could not even confirm the dates. I was helpless amongst these scribbles. I could see that many voices were present. Paragraphs showed distinct handwriting styles—slanted this way, slanted that way. Some timid. Some bold. Yet, still all squiggles. Scribbles. Helpless, indeed!

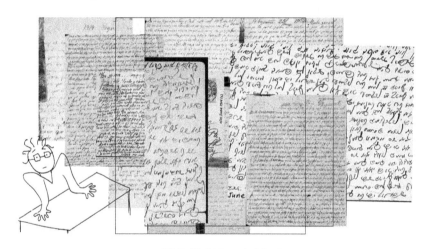

All Yiddish! I am helpless!

So I sought help. First there was Harry. I contacted Jewish Family Services and together we arranged I'd become a "friendly visitor" for Harry who lived alone, was 90, and wanted company. We agreed that during these weekly visits we'd read a Yiddish letter or two I'd bring. Of course, I enlarged them to make it easier for Harry. But Harry wasn't so interested. Reading Yiddish printed in the *Forward* was one thing, he said, "but all this lousy handwriting?!" He'd rather teach me to play chess. (Or give me a kiss or two.) Finally, it was clear, we weren't on the same page. So we decided to stop these visits.

Michal and Sam, in their 70s, could read the occasional letter I gave them in handwritten Hebrew. They were both born and raised in Israel. But Yiddish wasn't for them. They did manage to read one Yiddish letter, and to help with dates and to identify all the letter writers.

Then there was Ayn, age 92, elegant and kind, who taught Yiddish at a nearby temple. But who was stymied at every

First there was Harry.

turn. She did help me know which end of a letter was right-side-up, the date of the letter and, when on occasion someone had scratched a note in-between others, which note needed us to turn the letter upside-down in order to read it.

Finally I found, through YIVO (*Yidisher Visnshaftlekher Institut*), Caraid, a professional translator who had taken up the study of Yiddish in college and was part of a group of young people championing its vibrant literary legacy. These letters—after the usual greetings, after pleas for more correspondence, after God's blessings and well wishes—reveal details of the family my grandfather Eli left behind: his wife, Manya, six children who ranged in age from the youngest (four years old, my father Niuma) to the oldest (14 years old, my uncle Isor). Manya, I learn quickly, wasn't left alone to cope. Two brothers (Mokha and Veniamin), a sister (Klara), her stepmother Miriam, and her father Liev

Michal and Sam

all lived in the same village as she, the
village of Gorodische which was about
100 miles south of the city of Kiev.

There were gaps, important gaps.
I wanted to know more. Eli went to
America, left his family and his business
behind. What was this business he left
behind? A shop, but what products did
they sell? Was it
a general mercantile store? Did the shop
carry consistent inventory? Where was it
located? In a typical town square type
marketplace in Gorodische? Some of
these questions were answered later.

*Ayn: Often she helped me know
which side of a letter
was right-side-up.*

What I did learn from these Yiddish
letters however is that Eli had debts
the family wanted to pay off, and that
revenue from the retail shop business had been a traditional source
of family income. Manya bought and sold for the shop in Gorodische,
and also sold goods at marketplaces elsewhere: in particular the
nearby larger town of Smela.

After Eli left, Manya's brother Mokha took on the mantle of
responsibility for Manya's family. He knew the shop business. At the
same time his position in the local beet factory enabled him to get
Manya's eldest son, Isor, a job there as well. So Isor works, Manya minds
the shop. The other four children engage in their studies: religious and
secular.

From Manya:

*Isor is working at the factory as is Mokha. I sit minding the shop. . .
I don't know why I have the few little loaves of bread left and
bashekles [hooded scarves used by the Russian army] and still
twenty pairs of shoes to sell. . . Your children are well. With God's
blessing we will be together again.*

My Cast of characters 1914

Manya's Father, Liev Polansky

Mokha (her brother)

Veniamin (another brother)

Manya

Klara (her sister)

Isor (her eldest son, age 14)

Riva (her oldest daughter age 10)

Meer (her second oldest son, age 12)

Ita (age 8)

Iosif (age 6)

me (in 2014)

Niuma (my Dad) age 4

1914
Eli has left for America

MY CAST OF CHARACTERS

Manya • Klara • Riva • Liev • Ita • Mokha • Veniamin • Isor
Meer • Iosif • Niuma • Me

1/13 December 1914

Two Calendars—Gregorian and Julian

At the time these postcards and letters were written there were two calendars in use: Russia under the Tsars used the Julian calendar but the Western world used the Gregorian calendar. That is why there are two dates on every letter and every postcard written to Eli from his family: the date the Russians used at the time and the date—thirteen days later—which would be the date the Americans used.

Also notice that Americans and Russians (and Europeans) use (to this day) a different way of denoting calendar dates. In Europe and Russia the day comes first, then month, then year. The postcard you see was posted in Gorodische on 2.12.14. Thus the postcard (written on December 1st) was posted on December 2nd. For Americans? the month comes first, then day, then year.

It's easy to get confused, and this difference still exists.

2. Gone to America

The town where Eli left his family is Gorodische. Gorodische is in Kiev Province. The City of Kiev is its capitol. In 1914, Kiev was the regional administrative headquarters for the Imperium's three southern border provinces located west of the River Dnieper (Kiev, Podoliya, Vohlniya). The city of Kiev was also the regional *military* headquarters for the Tsar's Imperial Southwestern Armies. In other words, Kiev was Russia's major city in a border region across which—at that time—was Russia's enemy, the Austro-Hungarian Empire in control of Galicia (allied with a most aggressive neighbor, the German Empire) and readying to attack. And Gorodische, Manya's town, was just south of Kiev, connected to it by a major rail line.

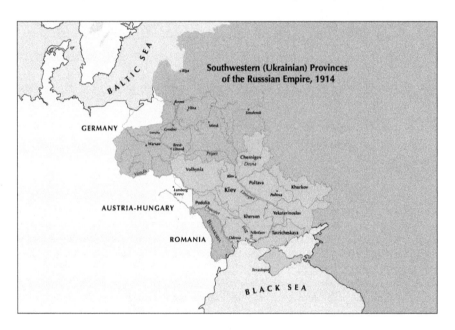

In August 1914, just two months after Eli has left, Russia, provoked by German aggression in Poland, declared war on the German and the Austro-Hungarian Empires, effectively entering the First World War. Tsar Nicolas II sends orders to his military headquarters in Kiev to intensify troop preparations for the tasks of war on Russia's

16

southwestern flank. That meant preparations for an armed offensive against Austro-Hungarian armies bunkered in Galicia (a swath of territory wedged between Russian Ukraine and Russian dominated Poland), and now controlled by the Austro-Hungarian empire.

These early letters to Eli just months after he has left for America are slight on details. Manya evades much mention of the shock of war. But a letter to Eli from a friend doesn't mince words: *It is very bad here.*

They have taken everything they can take. There is no business to be had. Everything is stopped. In the same letter Liev Polonsky, Manya's father (my great grandfather), writes: *What can I write to you that should be good? Nothing is good. It's difficult to write about. Only God, may His name be blessed, can help the children of Israel.* And so, too, Manya reveals her hopes and her fears: *Father says God will help as you will earn money there and send us some rubles.*

It takes four months before members of the family decide to start writing in Russian. They must have guessed that since Yiddish was more difficult, if not impossible, for the censor to read, its use delayed and maybe even prevented their letters to Eli from going forward, or his letters from arriving. There could well have been a bias against Yiddish (the "Jewish language"). Some authorities were all too eager to believe the wartime rumors that Jews might not be loyal to the Tsar and even might be spies for the enemy. Thus another reason to prevent or delay correspondence.

Finally, in November 1914, Eli received two letters mostly in Russian. On the front page of the letter of November 17 Manya writes in Yiddish. As before, she sticks to events and matters close to her heart and responsibilities: the children's well-being and always the anxieties when letters don't arrive from Eli. *I got the letter that you sent to Meir in Palestine. But your letters are four and even five weeks apart. What suffering this causes us. . . . About the shop, we bought some hand mirrors to sell which will interest quite nicely the little wives whose husbands are scarce and who come in often. . . . I still go to Smela to trade.*

On the back side of this letter to my surprise is *Dear Papa*—in Russian. Six times! There is a paragraph or a sentence or a fragment from each of the children. First, Isor and Meer in beautiful Russian script, then Riva and Ida and Iosif, and then there he was! My dad, a little boy of four, his bold signature, HIOMA (Niuma), capitalized, along with an unsuccessful attempt to copy his older brother's phrase: "I greet you."

The youngest children—Ita (eight years old), Iosif (six years), Niuma (four years)—each write the same sentence: I greet you.

FROM ISOR: *(the oldest now 14 years old)*
'*Dear Papa. At the shop trading is little. Mother buys some goods at 10 to 15 rubles and sells them at other marketplaces at sometimes six times their cost. The rest of the goods she sells at good prices. Uncle Veniamin brings her goods from Cherkassy to sell, thus he comes often to Gorodische.*'

FROM MEER: *(12 years old)*
'*Dear Papa! . . . I am studying with religious teacher and I wish you success, happiness, health and that we can be together again soon.*'

FROM RIVA: *(now ten years old)*
'*Dear Papa . . . I have a new coat. I wish you good health.*'

The moment I saw my father's penned sentence, *Dear Papa, I greet you*, written in Russian cursive, I was smitten. Instantly smitten. My Dad had long passed by the time I got to this sentence, but there he was and I was with him! We were going to be together on a most intriguing adventure into another time, era, land, family, and culture. He would lead the way. We had become very close the last ten or so years of his life. He was supportive of my work. We both had the writing habit. Smitten I was. Translation was a trudge: handwriting styles differ, calendars differ, the written alphabet before 1917 differs somewhat from the modern Russian style I knew; places changed names, dates are written differently, the names of any one person vary from the formal, the diminutive, the nickname, to the ways one shows endearment. *All* this sometimes in Yiddish, sometimes in Russian. I was going pretty much solo in terms of real bodies to help me. But this is where I wanted to be, this is what I wanted to be doing: being with my father when he was a young boy; reading the beautiful calligraphy of his oldest brother Isor for content and meaning; finding so many writers sending their greetings on one postcard, putting in sentences wherever they could fit, along the margins, upside down, even in between the lines of another!

Once deciphered, I found patterns emerging from the different letter writers. My grandmother Manya writes matter of factly, and almost exclusively about what is happening in the family. Her siblings and father, and her eldest son, Isor, write about other matters. The rules for the male writers have been established. The letters to Eli are to remain matter-of-fact, calm, and if possible cheery, in order not to worry Eli but also because all letters had to pass a military censor. Isor did this best.

From Isor:

Dear Papa,

Before I was working at the receiving department of the beet plant, but now I am in the office where they weigh the juice and the starch/ syrup.

Sometimes, however, Liev (Manya's father) and her sister, Klara, are more to the point.

From Liev:

Your letter arrived without a stamp. When you write, include the stamp . . . . Nothing good is happening. There is nothing to write about the war. Of course you read about it too. And you probably know we are also at war with the Turks. It is very difficult to describe in detail. Only God should help. The want is great and the lack is also great. It is impossible to earn money. Therefore, God, blessed be His name, should help you earn well so that you can send us money. You will send money from America. No money here and no merchandise. We paid off the debts we are aware of.

From Klara:

There are several hundred Jewish reservists here in Gorodische. In February there will be another mobilization after which there will be few young men left. Inflation is terrible. The mood is heavy. War is horrible. No one has mercy for anyone. There is nothing to be done. Everywhere there is only one word heard, war.

Besides reporting facts of managing her household, all of Manya's letters reveal her deep wish to reunite with Eli. *God grant that we see each other soon. God wish you success so that we can be together soon. . . Perhaps you will be able to be here for Passover.* Whether the plans had included Eli returning to Gorodische—permanently or to gather the whole family for a new home in the United States—Manya's wish to be reunited with her husband and the wishes of her children to be reunited with their father were not to be fulfilled for another eight very long years. War. Revolution. Civil War. More war.

Pogroms. Famine. Like the plagues at Passover.

A LETTER TO PAPA

It is Saturday night. The sun had set and the Sabbath had past. But still my mother didn't light the kerosene lamp.

"If I don't write tonight, God knows when I'll have time," my mother said. She reached for the lamp, took it carefully apart, cleaned the wick, wiped the glass chimney with a cloth, and filled the lamp with fresh kerosene. She lit the wick and turned the flame, green and orange and blue, up high. She reached for a piece of writing paper, the inkwell, and a penholder with a steel nib, and placed them on the table.

She and I were the only ones at home.

"Maybe I can have a few minutes of peace to write to your father," she said, and soon her pen began to move across the page. I could hear the scratching. I liked this time of the week. I knew that I would be writing to my father on the same sheet of paper and wondered whether I could stay awake until my mother finished.

I fell asleep.

The next day, my mother asked me to sit at the table, to be careful not to spill the ink nor to splotch the paper with my pen.

"Here, Numele," she said, "add your regards to this letter and then I can mail it."

I looked at the sheet of paper. My mother's handwriting, in Yiddish, filled one side of the sheet. On the other side, I could see the bold handwriting of my brother Mayor [Meer], the fine girlish script of Becky [Rivka] and Ida, and finally the sprawling letters of my brother Joseph [Iosif]. I wasn't too much interested in what they said. I knew their "regards" by heart, and I knew that each week they said the same thing.

Now and then, however, my older brother and sisters mentioned their school work. "I got a 4 in history," Becky might say. And Ida might write, "My teacher gave me a 5 in geography." They were bragging about their high marks.

I looked at the sheet again. As usual, there was just about an inch or two of white space left at the bottom for me. That was enough. I wrote:

"Dear Papa. I am, thank God, alive and well, hoping to hear the same from you. We miss you. Now I'll say goodbye. Your loving son, Benyomin"

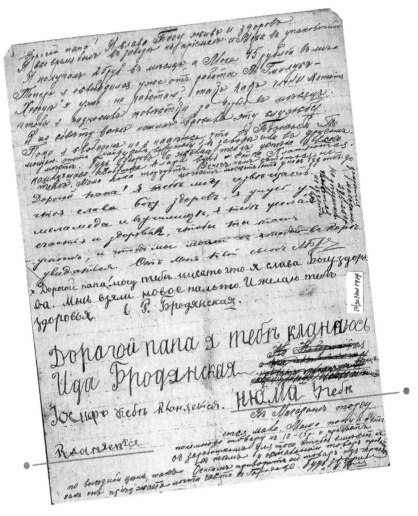

'I GREET YOU'

old style   new style

цѣна   цена

сѣть   сеть

вѣтеръ   ветер

Manya = Mali, Masha

Mokha = Mardko, Mordecai, Max

Isor = Essor, Asher, Seryosha

Rivka = Sarah, Sonya

Niuma = Numele, Niumochka, Benny

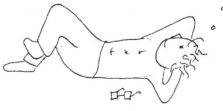

3. WAR DISRUPTS

*W*hen Eli left for America, before Russia entered World War I, Manya's family was rather well off living in Gorodische, a prosperous town unlike so many other villages in the Pale at the time. Gorodische had a fully operational beet sugar factory, a department store, and a rail connection. The Znamenka-Fastov rail line connected Gorodische to nearby Smela, the locale of another beet sugar processing plant, and beyond that a short distance to Cherkassy, a larger trading center on the Dnieper River with 40,000 inhabitants, many of them Jews.

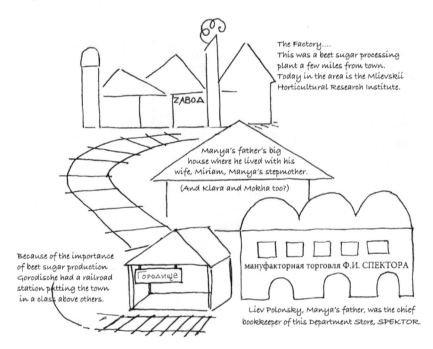

The Factory....
This was a beet sugar processing plant a few miles from town. Today in the area is the Mlievskii Horticultural Research Institute.

ZABOA

Manya's father's big house where he lived with his wife, Miriam, Manya's stepmother.

(And Klara and Mokha too?)

Because of the importance of beet sugar production Gorodische had a railroad station putting the town in a class above others.

Городище

мануфакторная торговля Ф.И. СПЕКТОРА

Liev Polonsky, Manya's father, was the chief bookkeeper of this Department Store, SPEKTOR.

The Town of Gorodische.

True, it was the Russian Pale into which we were all stuffed, suffocating from lack of opportunity and from rules, rules, constraints, constraints. But the family was not doing badly. Manya's brother, Mokha, is connected to the local beet plant. (The plant is possibly

24

owned by a Jewish entrepreneur from Kiev. Jews owned several of the largest beet factories in Russia.) Besides his own employment there Mokha manages to get employment for Isor, Manya's oldest son, and on a seasonal basis for other various relatives too. Russia was the world's second highest producer of beet sugar just behind Germany according to statistics available for 1910. And Kiev Province was Russia's leader in beet sugar production.

In addition, Manya's father had an important position in town which could not but favor the family. He was chief bookkeeper for a large department store, SPEKTOR. We see the stationery Manya often used is from СПЕКТОР (SPEKTOR). (Even now there is a SPEKTR Department Store in Kiev.) But two questions remain: was the store in Gorodische one of several within the province? Was Liev the highest ranking officer of the branch in Gorodische? We do know that Liev's house was one of only a few that had electricity.

The stationery Manya often used is from SPEKTOR

My father's family was educated. Manya was literate in Yiddish and in Russian. The family as best it can was taking on the duties and finances of running the retail trade business that Eli left behind. Manya, her brother Mokha, her father Liev and her son Isor in the early letters report on the goods they are selling, the debts that are owed, the merchants they deal with; the need to pay off the debts owed and later, as we shall see, the need to close the business down. Manya's own trading activities, going out of town to other fairs, often took her to nearby Smela. Her brother Veniamin—a dentist in the busy port city of Cherkassy on the Dnieper River—supported her in her business by acquiring tradable goods there and bringing them to her.

In sum, Manya's family's economic position in 1914 derives from Eli's retail trade business, wages from factory employment, Liev's position as chief bookkeeper and her brother Veniamin's earnings as a dentist.

But we also know that war disrupts, intervenes. War stops normal factory production, insisting on new purposes for the factory's machines and buildings. Military needs get priority. Soldiers need barracks. Soldiers need clothing. Authorities need supplies for the military, and confiscate inventories of anything and everything they find. Authorities print money—to pay soldiers, to buy supplies that can't be confiscated, and to buy armaments. That creates inflation.

The life of a town is turned upside down to meet the needs of the military. *Everything is stopped. They have taken everything they can take. There is no business to be had,* writes Eli's friend. The family knew Eli's business could no longer function as it once did for there would be no goods to sell. *Demand is high, but supply is scarce,* writes Liev.

How long would the factory keep producing beet sugar? What about conscription? Isor is still too young. Liev is too old. Manya's brother, Veniamin, is conscripted in September. Mokha, we have to assume, will soon be conscripted as well.

Despite all this, Hanukkah in 1914 is a cheery affair. My grandmother Manya and her brother Mokha keep to the set protocol to prevent Eli from feeling too much their worries.

From Mokha:

> . . . *Despite the fact that we haven't heard from you, we keep our promise to write. We are at home with Manya making merry because it's Hanukkah and the children have their Hanukkah money, I was able to get a job for Seryosha [Isor] at the beet sugar factory. Your brother Chaim has work in Ekaterinoslav, thanks also to yours truly. We are impatient to hear from you.*

From Manya:

> . . . *Your mother came with Hanukkah money of three rubles. In a word we are all fine. Seryosha isn't home right now. He is at the factory. The children greet you. They are already asleep. I kiss you.*

I can imagine a Hanukkah party but I wonder what their menorah would have looked like? Simple? Ornate? Small? Large? Almost one hundred years after these letters were written, I visited the Jewish Museum of Switzerland in Basel, a small museum just right for a beginner like me.

An 18th century menorah I saw at the Jewish Museum of Switzerland in Basel.

I say "just right for a beginner like me" because except for Hanukkah and menorahs, Passover and seder plates, the *ketubah* of my daughter's marriage, and the *mezzuzahs* for (other) peoples' doorways, there were lots of things new to me in this museum. Torah mantles, for instance, all decorated with the same two Hebrew letters under a crown. These letters must signify something I was certain, but my young teenager guides couldn't tell me. I saw boxes. "Tefillin box cover," the labels read. The box covers had interesting designs but I knew not then what purpose these boxes served.

* * * * *

GRANDFATHER'S HOUSE

There were five electric bulbs in my grandfather's house. They were located in the corridor, in the dining room, in the kitchen and in two of the bed rooms. The light came on Tuesday and Thursday, at sunset. It was a magical sight. I tried to be at Grandfather's big house on Tuesdays and Thursdays and could hardly wait until the electric bulbs would begin to glow, first faintly, and then with full power, spreading a white light into every corner of the room. Now it's Thursday, a few minutes before sundown. I look out the large window of Grandfather's house and I see people walking slowly, some stopping and looking at the house.

"Why are they looking this way?" I ask my aunt Klara, who was with me.

"They want to see the electric light."

Soon, more and more people come by and stop on the sidewalk across from the house. It is getting dark outside; and inside, too, it was becoming gloomy. I began to be afraid.

"Aunt Klara, when? When, Aunt Klara?"

"I don't know. We'll have to wait until they turn the power on at the central electric station."

I liked those words: "central electric station." They sounded important. And grandfather's house was important because it was connected with wires to that place – where was it? – that sent out the light.

The crowd outside grew a little bigger; two peasants stopped with their horse and wagon; people with big bundles put them down on the ground and strained their necks toward the house.

Then I saw the faint glow of light in the bulb hanging by a wire over the dining room table. Very slowly it grew brighter and then the whole house was lit up. I looked outside. The light came out through the open windows and seemed to touch the people. Some stood with their mouths open. Others spread out their arms in wonder. Some shook their heads; they couldn't believe that a little glass bulb, without kerosene and wick, could give ten times more light than their own lamps at home.

Suddenly, all was black in the house. Aunt Klara rushed over to me, saying, "Don't be afraid. Something went wrong at the central electric station."

She hurried over to the window, leaned out and said something to the crowd.

I could hear a gentle, sad murmur coming from the street into the house.

"Is it possible the devils have gotten into the central electric station?" one man shouted at Aunt Klara. "I don't know. I don't know. Something went wrong and cut off our power. But please don't go away. I have music for you."

It was a warm evening and the moon was out in a clear sky. The people didn't want to leave. A sweet aroma of apple blooms came from Grandfather's garden.

Aunt Klara moved a table close to the open window. She carried a small phonograph from the back room and placed it on the table. She cranked the handle. Then she placed a record on the machine and turned the phonograph horn toward the window.

It was the "Anvil's Chorus," and the people outside burst into applause. Then they listed silently, swaying their bodies slowly to the ringing of the blacksmith's hammer.

When it was over the people shouted, "Again! Again!" Aunt Klara played it over and over again. Then she came to the window, spread out her arms, and said: "Please, you must go now."

My Jewish education ceased when I was ten, after my parents' first separation. Until then we lived in Washington D.C. amongst my mother's aunts and uncles. I remember my weekly task: *Elisa, walk over to Aunt Rose. She has shmaltz for us.* I remember being Queen Esther at Purim, the taste of *hamentaschen*, Passovers with lots of cousins. I remember some Yiddish: my father and my mother singing to us children the exquisitely beautiful lullaby *Oifn Prepatchik* which I listen to this day for a soothing oh so soothing memory.

I grew up in a rooming house my mother managed with pride. I would often help her bundle the sheets that came off the beds of the lodgers. With one of the sheets opened wide on the floor, counting as I put others in, I would then tie two of four corners together then the other two, slipping in a ticket with the total number of sheets to be washed and pressed. This, a happy memory. I remember putting the sign "Room for Rent" in our window when a vacancy came open. And playing "I am mother" at her desk in the living room. She was happy running this business from that desk. I was happy alongside her. Playing "I am mother" for me meant repeatedly exploring the contents of the two vertical drawers each the size of a book that bracketed the inkwell stand. Two drawers full of magical playthings that I could empty out, sort through then put back: stamps of all functions (ration stamps, coupons, postage stamps) and other secrets of success. Not unlike a jewel box I might have played with knowing the joy that mother feels when she is looking to wear some earrings or a necklace or a brooch that are also magical and bring happiness to the world.

In 1929, at the age of 19, my mother left Omaha to seek work in Washington D.C., where she joined her cousins, aunts and uncles. It was easy then for her to find a job. She had come from a family where intelligence was used, where intelligence led, where intelligence mattered. Overshadowed by her wild and raucous younger sister Tillie Lerner (Olsen), nonetheless, my mother Jann knew her intellectual abilities, her powers. She spent the years before children and the first four years after children as a secretary at the Department of the Navy. When the family grew to include my parents, a four-year old, and a baby (me), but before my brother was born, she resigned. Her job history shows the reason, "unable to secure domestic help."

After my birth, "inadequate treatment" made us both ill. My mother's doctor advised her to get care and to get help from her relatives. She took my sister and me to Omaha, Nebraska for rest with her parents. That this was a separation from my father is also possible. There had been marital trouble between them even before we were born. While we were staying in Omaha, Jann's discussions with her two D.C. aunts begat the idea of her owning and running a rooming house. When her Aunt Rose both found an appropriate house and lent her the required money for its purchase, she decided to return.

Yes, there *was* happiness in that rooming house. My father's voice full of song as he and Mr. Grusky, one of the roomers who played the piano, sent music to the second floor often just at our bedtimes. My favorite songs (that I sing to this day): *Wraggle Taggle Gypsies, The Anniversary Waltz, Water Boy*. Other happiness: when my mother would be dressing to go dancing with my father. Also our family outings to Rock Creek Park (which we called "Scream and Yell" for that is what we did), going afterwards to the Polar Bear Ice Cream Parlor for frozen custard.

But their fights were ferocious. I had the bedroom next to theirs. My sister's room was far away at the other end of a long hallway. My brother's next to hers. My mother had decided my brother and I had to have our separate bedrooms. Such a lonely place—my "own" bedroom. How lonely I was. Maybe my mother thought this was best. But that move from one room to another meant leaving the comfort of being with my brother to the go-it-alone-ness of having to listen to the fights of my parents—without understanding anything but the fierceness of the emotions.

OUR D.C. ROOMING HOUSE

Soon after you were born in November 1941, America entered World War II. Hospitals were short-handed of doctors and nurses. Inadequate treatment made us both ill for several months.

We were living in Washington Park then isolated because of gas shortages and we couldn't get to the doctors for medical attention. This was a Catholic area and we were the only Jewish family. I began to realize that my four- year old (your sister Molly) was having problems socializing with other children in the neighborhood; that my immediate neighbor's husband was a strict Catholic and had issued a ruling his children were not to play with my children. My neighbor, despite her husband's order, helped me because I was sick. She took me to her doctor. The doctor said I needed care and to get help from my relatives. That I ought not to be working.

I needed to work. How could I quit my job? How could I not work, stay home take care of my kids and yet make enough money to help support the family financially? My aunt suggested a rooming house as the only thing to do and my other aunt also knew about these things and so she found the house and I allowed her to put 1000 dollars, unseen on a three-level row house in an unpretentious and conventional neighborhood in northwest Washington.

A three-story house would be ideal for a rooming house (for gentlemen only) and provide an income that might not replace entirely my salary at the Navy Department but adequately allow us to live modestly. I had two young children and I wanted them to have a mother at home. The times were favorable. The government was expanding. Citizens were looking for civil service jobs because every department of the government was enlarging due to the war crisis. Young single men needed lodging.

We lived on the first floor, renting rooms on the second and third. When I paid off my loan we moved our bedrooms to the second floor. We were a total of eight roomers on the third floor and, after your brother was born, the five of us. Thirteen in all.

In the Words of Jann Lerner Brodinsky

WHAT MAKES A GOOD MOTHER?

It seems to me that it is not for me to decide what I want to do—but how best to do it. I already have my job: it is to be a good mother and wife. I know the requirements of a good wife. Some of the requirements I do not fulfill as well as I would like, but I know what they are. But I am not so clear in my mind as to the requirements of a good mother.

In determining these requirements the first years of a child's life can be dismissed. Firstly, I know the mother's role here pretty well. Secondly, my children are now passing beyond that state, and I must prepare for the next: the school child, or the child from five to 12.

What does the child of this age group need. What makes a mother most satisfying to him during this period when he is learning so much, and beginning to feel so confident of himself and his own abilities.

Does the mother add something to a child's background by having a job outside the home? Does this really enlarge her interests? Does this make her interesting to her children and make them more confident of her wisdom? A mother's function is to be there when her children need advice or help— to serve as a background which will stimulate and inspire her children to develop to the utmost of their abilities in the best interests of mankind, to be self-reliant and independent thinkers.

What does "background" mean? Do the children need the example of a mother who has friends and well-directed conversation among them? Do they need the example of mother reading, or mother playing the piano or of mother helping the neighbors.

Is it bad for them to see mother at home, always cooking, washing, ironing, rarely going out, the household drudge? It is it better to be a mother who cannot cook, who lets the house go — but who has a job or who plays the piano, or who plays games with them and is jolly fun?

* * * * *

4. INFLATION SPIRALS

$\mathcal{A}s$ 1915 progressed, notwithstanding the plagues of war (conscription, capture, imprisonment), Manya's family stayed intact. The men—her father Liev, her brothers Mokha, Veniamin, and her son Isor were all working. Manya's five youngest children—Meer, Rivka, Ita, Iosif, and Niuma—all studying. Although Manya's brother Veniamin now is in the army and posted to a military hospital in nearby Cherkassy, he continues to help out. At first, the complaints seem to be mostly about the length of time the family waits for letters from Eli. All the family note the length of time a letter would take to

Brother Mokha (unmarried) works at the Factory (a wheeler-dealer type)

Manya's Father, Liev Polansky, Chief Bookkeeper at Department Store in town

Isor, Manya's eldest son (14 years old) also works at the Factory

Sister Klara (unmarried)

Brother Veniamin, Dentist (married to Liuba)

Manya's 5 Pillars of Support after Eli leaves for America (1914)

get from Eli in America to them in Gorodsiche. *What's happened?* writes Veniamin, *it's been two and a half months without a word from you. We know it is not entirely your doing, but all the same, in order to get words from you, write more often.* Mokha: *Your last letter took 10 weeks to arrive.* Again, Mokha: *Your long awaited letter took 40 days to arrive.* The fact that my grandmother was surrounded by her family had to have helped her to cope with her worries and excruciatingly long gaps between Eli's letters. The reason for these delays, to some extent, was military censorship of mail.

I am looking at a postcard which identifies a Petrograd Censor. The date the postcard to Eli was posted in Gorodische is June 8, 1916. The date it passed the Petrograd Censor was June 26. That's an *additional* delay of two and one-half weeks beyond the *normal* 21-28 day delivery time for mail. If Eli's letters from America suffered the same routing and process, no wonder letters took so long.

More often, however, the letters from Manya were about her need for Eli to send money. These requests were within the bounds of civility and in addition to her wish to show her caring for him.

From Manya:

I am getting ready for Passover, I have already, thank God, finished with all of the preparations but how can I go on with Passover knowing that you are alone, without us and we are without you. If we live, may we be together again. . . Send us money, I use all of Isor's earnings. Thank God he has earned more than a 100 rubles. I have no money.

Isor explains further:

Dear Papa:
At the moment [April, 1915] I am without work but within days I will be working again. I am using my free time to study with Mokha, especially foreign languages, accounting etc. Mama's note to you to send us money is more to satisfy Grandfather than something we really need. Our material situation in general is okay. The selling of some remaining goods, my salary, and payments from former buyers who have owed you money usually satisfy our needs. Still since this is now my second month at home I am aware that we are drawing down our capital reserve. Of course it would be much better to live with your earnings and if you have excess don't hesitate to send us money.

A letter from Mokha points to inflation as the culprit for their increasing needs:

We were surprised and even worried because you mentioned you were ill. Don't keep anything from us. Why do you write so little about your life? Write how you live, what kind of earnings you make and what these are in general in America. It seems in a few days, using the Hebrew calendar it will be one year since you arrived in America.

*Prices are rising, and we are stocking up on wood and sugar etc.
Isor yesterday went to pick up wood for us from the factory's forest
lands. I bought some sugar recently for resale and perhaps I'll earn
as much as 30 to 40 rubles.*

No other news. Be well.

Manya's requests that Eli send them money were successful. The
first receipt of forty rubles arrived in June 1915. Unfortunately, however, the occasional money order from Eli doesn't begin to match the
consequences of price inflation now rampant in war time Russia. Prices
were going up by multiples month after month. Five months after the
family first receives Eli's money order in rubles, Manya, Liev, and Isor
are all now unequivocal. They need more of Eli's monetary help.

From Isor:

*We have received now a total of 140 rubles from you. Today
[November, 1915] I learned that I will stay working with the
deliveries of the pressed beet leftovers. Price inflation is like nothing
ever before. Prices are rising to an impossible 3 to 4 times. In
a word, nothing here to be proud of. Lucky are those who do not have
to know of our life here.*

*The letter you wrote about your coming here none of us liked.
[Uncle] Veniamin wrote you a whole letter in which he advised that
we go there instead. He tried, in as much as the situation here is
worsening, to dissuade you from coming. He wrote that Grandfather
is in complete agreement with us and does not support this
action.*

*Grandfather has 75 rubles left from the store. At first we lived
from our earnings from the store. Then from my earnings and now
from your money. Grandfather has not given any of his personal
monies to us. You are envied not only because you don't have war
but in all things. Your postcards come often enough now. Now the
dollar is worth anything from 3 to 16 rubles. It's a good time to send
dollars. Better more often and in smaller quantities, 25 to 35 dollars
per month is good.*

To that letter Liev, Manya's father, adds: *All is very expensive What used to cost 10 kopeks now costs 30, or worse. Send money more often and in more amounts. It's needed. Send as much money as you can.* And just one month later [December 1915], he writes: *Not much is good. Our family situation is very bad. That which cost 30 kopeks now is four times more. Manya needs not 40 rubles but 100 rubles. Send as much money as you can.*

Let's think of Eli's position as he received these urgent requests to send more money, that all Manya's rubles were being used up to buy an ever-*decreasing* basket of goods. As long as Eli went through official channels to send money and didn't try illicit methods, he had to buy rubles with his dollars at the official, fixed rate of one dollar for three rubles. Thus, at a foreign exchange dealer, he paid the official rate: if he wanted to send Manya 100 rubles, he would have to buy them at the *official rate*—one dollar buys 3 rubles—which is fixed. And so he paid $33 (plus $4 fee) to send her 100 rubles.

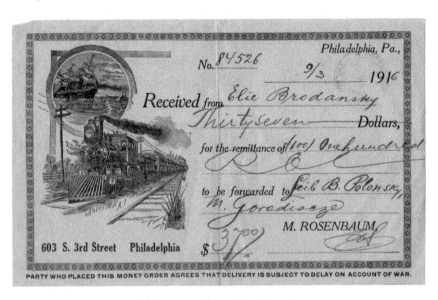

Eli's money order to Liev Polonsky.

If Eli could send dollars directly (as Isor requests) the *unofficial exchange rate would beget many more rubles.* Isor writes: *Now the dollar is worth anything from 3 to 16 rubles. It's a good time to send dollars. Better more often and in smaller quantities, 25 to 35 dollars per month is good.*

If Eli's dollar could get 16 rubles instead of only 3, then his $37 could bring the family almost 600 rubles, not 100. *Send dollars,* Isor is urging, perhaps unable to understand the intricacies of the international financial system and the situation of currency exchange between Russia and its allies during wartime. But working *unofficially* wasn't possible for Eli to accomplish. Sending dollars in an envelope would never get to the family. Sending dollars hidden in a trusted-someone's pockets or shoes or inner seams might, but that doesn't seem to have happened. So Eli spends $37 dollars (going with the official exchange rate) when he can to send the family 100 rubles. And Manya's reply is always that it is not enough.

From Manya:

You write that I try to spend less, about this I can report the following: As you know before you started to send me money I tried to adhere to a budget for food and shelter of 50 rubles all summer, not taking into account expenses for the children's education and clothing. But that wasn't enough, I had to spend the earnings of Isor from last winter, and what I made from trading.

This summer Isor earned 40 rubles, 25 to 30 out of which I used to fix the roof which had been damaged by the wind. Isor has worked now for two months at the factory and received 30 rubles and still all of that and all the 140 rubles which you have sent have been spent and I still am not able to buy either for myself or for the children clothes and shoes.

Even now when I received your 60 rubles, I could not get what the children need because there isn't even enough money for food and shelter. Besides that, Isor needs a coat, as he is going around in a two-year old winter coat. For the education of Iosif, Ita, Riva, and Meer, I spend more than 8 rubles a month.

Isor is so busy at the factory that he has no time to study and has a room at the factory where he sleeps and comes home 1 or 2 times a week. The factory is very satisfied with Isor's work and with God's help he will work there until Spring. He could have had about

300 rubles by now but gives all his money to me for expenses and spends not one kopek on himself.

As you can see not only is there no money left from what I can get but it will be difficult to make ends meet this winter. Firewood at 23 kopeks per pud. Instead of a coat for Isor I am buying wood, and galoshes for Iosif (for 3 rubles, 40 kopecks). Coats for Iosif, Niuma, and Meer I have sewn from your clothes. They are neat and cleanly dressed, just not in new clothing.

Manya says she can't make ends meet with what he sends and she's only spending for food and shelter. Money to pay for all her expenses, she writes, depends on Isor's salary, whatever money she makes from trading, and whatever Eli sends. But, she adds, it is never enough.

Eli was in a fix. At the official exchange rate, to double the rubles they would receive, he would have to come up with twice as many dollars. His brother writing to him from Palestine in January 1916 congratulated him for doubling his salary in one year: that he was now earning twice what he had been earning a year before: *instead of 3 to 4 dollars a week, you are earning 8 to 10 dollars a week.* But Eli knew even with these earnings, one month of salary would be required to send Manya 100 rubles. Could he really spare his whole salary every month, and leave nothing for himself?

Eli earned his wages by working as a peddler, not unlike other young Jewish men who came to America to seek a better life. He peddled dry goods. Peddling was the customary first job for Jewish immigrants from Eastern Europe. I suppose if you take the argument that brokering and trading of goods and monies was our historical work as authorities refused us the right to practice so many other economic professions, then what the peddler was doing in America was similar to what he or she had been doing in Eastern Europe for centuries: making markets. I am reminded of Gluckel of Hameln's memoir written in the late 1600s. After her husband died she took on his business of trading in diamonds and other precious jewels, traveled the European continent far and wide (and bore 12 children!). In Eli's case, instead of diamonds or foods or wines, he was learning what the householder/housewife around Wilmington, Delaware, wanted, and spent his time getting her those things. The peddler in early twentieth century America was an important itinerant shopkeeper for many households, especially those in rural areas. The further he went the peddler created supply lines that hadn't existed before.

Eli, the Peddler

Eli seems to have been caught between the demands he is receiving from Manya to send more money, the official, fixed exchange rate which limited the amount of rubles dollars can buy, his need to buy a horse and cart, and having enough on which to live. No wonder that being so far from his loved ones and at the same time being asked so much by them leads to depression. *I was upset to hear you aren't feeling well,* writes Manya in January 1916. *Don't work so much and don't fret about money. Eat well. Drink milk.*

Eli's dilemma

In an especially poignant note Isor writes:

> *We got your postcard in which you seemed unhappy which caused us to suffer. But really, what's important is that we have hope that things will get better. Hope. That is the pillar of life. Eat better food. Don't fret about money. Don't worry about us. Have hope. Get well. Take care of yourself. Don't get depressed. Everything will be okay. Again, don't worry because when a person is sick and then gets depressed that just becomes a second illness. Certainly buy yourself a horse and cart to make things easier. At least you will be able to sell and have your own earnings. Be patient. Don't sink into depression.*

Manya too:

> *I am very upset that you wrote that you can't work. I beg you to buy a delivery horse and cart. Don't get yourself into a state of missing us. It's not good for you.*

28 Dec 1915—back of envelope with Nikitankin Military Censor Stamp.

5. Scythe against Stone

I don't know when the fights started, or the reasons. Perhaps my father didn't want to move out of Washington, D.C. to Bethesda, Maryland. Perhaps he had already made contact with Mary, who was to become his second wife less than a decade later. Perhaps he had not found an appropriate way to get along with my mother. Nor wanted to. Perhaps he *was* inconsiderate. Perhaps they *were* scythe against stone. (This was a phrase my father used when, as an adult, I questioned him about their relationship.) In a letter to him early in his marriage, before any of us, his children, were born, his eldest brother Isor (now Anglicized Oscar)—as close to a family authority as is possible, ten years his elder, and the hero of the family's much desired emigration from Russia—excoriates my father for the marital troubles with my mother which are due, in Oscar's opinion, to my father's lack of consideration.

January 19, 1936

Dear Ben,

Please understand I'm not trying to be too personal, but I would like to exchange opinions with you in regard to your driftings on the matrimonial sea.

According to certain hints on the part of Mom, Pop, and your brother Joe there seems to be a lack of harmony and unity between you and Jann who is in my eyes an extremely good, conscientious, willing to cooperate to the utmost, fine and dear girl. And I'm at a loss to understand why such a situation should prevail in your mutual relationship. In my opinion, such a state of affairs can be basically corrected if you only make a serious attempt in this direction. According to some information gathered from sources you show very little consideration for Jann and this is a terrific crime. [Emphasis, his.]

A thing so obvious and yet so obscure for many in the matrimonial business is: why not try to understand each other? You'll never regret pursuing such a policy. And as a rule small things are more aggravating than big ones. For instance, according to Mom and your brother Joe, those abusive visitings of your friends are going over every tolerable limit. You and Jann are working all day and with such practices you are deprived of the privilege to retire when and how desired. Why all this policy of breaking up a home? Why not dine at home at least once a day? Why not take your wife out at least once or twice a week without the company of friends? Why not cooperate? For without that life is HELL. [Emphasis his.]

Why not buy a regular bedroom suite? A studio couch is only good for an afternoon nap and to retire on it during the night is also hell: I have one and I know. Jann should have much more consideration in this respect because she works hard and absolutely needs plenty of rest. Perhaps I should have expounded a little longer on this subject. I'll close however by urging you heartily and with all the fibres of my soul to make a success of your married life. It may help your educational and literary ambitions.

Take care of yourself and love to you,

your devoted brother.

"*It may help your educational and literary ambitions,*" writes Oscar. Yes, from way back it was clear my father was an artist, not a businessman nor a scholar. More in temperament like his deceased brother Meer, he had the artist's eye, ear and hand. Visual, theatrical, poetic. His own reminiscences of his childhood point to this. Evenings listening to his brother Meer play the balalaika, his sister singing Russian love songs. . . . Drawing with the pencils on stiff white paper that Isor would bring from his work place. . . . His cousin Avrum telling him his pictures were "truly splendid."

Just a few years after arriving in the USA, my father was creating cartoons, writing plays and stories and submitting these to literary publications. And winning prizes. At the age of 13 and 14 he was publishing his stories in the *Idische Velt* (Yiddish World). At the age of 15 he won his first of several monetary prizes for cartoons he submitted to *St Nicholas* magazine, a well known literary publication for children.

He contributed his literary talents to the Workmen's Circle Youth Club. This is undoubtedly where he met my mother though there are no details about this.

When Oscar wrote his admonishing letter, my father by then had graduated from the University of Delaware where he had helped to create and was editor of a literary publication there, *The Humanist*. Finally, I mustn't omit what had to have been a morale and ego booster for this young ambitious literary man: his prize-winning essay in *The Forward* in January 11, 1931. He was 21 years old. First prize and $50 dollars for his essay, "I am a Jew and I am an American." My father's artistic life with friends of similar bent I am guessing didn't include my mother and yet wasn't going to be stopped.

Perhaps my father's lack of consideration *had* infected their marriage. Something was happening between my mother and father. Whatever it was, when I was ten years old, my mother decided it was time to move: for better schooling? for the fact that she didn't want her growing children living in a rooming house full of gentlemen? for a separation because the marriage wasn't working? Because the marriage was scythe against stone?

I can see now, only now, my mother had an ability to fend for herself and that is a strength that can cut—indeed like scythe against stone—both ways in marriage. She had made for herself a living with that rooming house (a business and a people place). My father may have wanted some other kind of partner or wife. My mother, I am guessing now, could not be the woman he *might have* loved.

So we moved to Bethesda, Maryland, a suburb of Washington, DC. The house was purchased in both of their names but a separation was at hand. We left our relatives behind in Washington, and with that I left behind the feeling of belonging to a large family of aunts, uncles, cousins, along with Jewish traditions and Jewish learning. For after that, instead of a familiar comfortable and enriching terrain, there was a barrenness, just the four of us—my mother and we three siblings. My school years after that were in communities where the majority of students were Christians and so were my friends. That's when I began to make up stories to tell folks what *I* got for Christmas even though Christmas wasn't a word we used at all in the month of December. Even in the classroom there was an exercise for each student to state what they got for Christmas (no different than what did you do during your summer vacation).

My father never lived with us in Bethesda. He immediately rented his own apartment near his office in D.C. My mother wasted no time finding work for herself. She went from job to job the first year until she secured a fine position as secretary to the Chief of the Department of Anesthesiology at the National Institutes of Health. My memories of our three years in Bethesda alone with our mother are contradictory. On the one hand, sad—because it seems that my mother loved my father. And they had separated. During this time, I learned later, he was engaged in an affair with a co-worker, Mary. Mary who he later married. I do not know if my mother knew that then but my recollection is clear: she would sit at the piano and sing, over and over:

> A song of love is a sad song, hi lilly, hi lilly hi lo.
> A song of love is a song of woe, for I have loved and I know.
> Hi lilli, hi lilli, hi lo, hi lo,
> Hi lilli , hi lilli hi lo.

And on the other hand, my mother was happy—when she would come home from a day at the work she loved and put her feet up against the wall for a few minutes before making dinner and I would be with her, my feet up the wall too. Happy with her. During one of those years, my brother and sister and I engaged in a special project for her birthday. It was to be a surprise and it was a very special project for me: to gather the funds (how I don't remember), to go with a neighbor to the clothing store and pick out a "topper" coat that she would like. I remember the yellow, nubby fabric. Perfect I thought to surprise her with this gift. Happy I was because she was happy, laughing at an office party, playing volley ball with her doctor boss and team mates. I was eleven years old.

6. Wrapping Tefillin

In August 1915 Manya's second oldest child, Meer, turned thirteen.

Dear Papa,

First of all I am alive and well and wish you the same. On Wednesday 12th of August, I will start wearing the tefillin. For now I will wear [Uncle] Max's [Mokha] but write me whether I should get my own because it costs five rubles.

The set of Cyrillic letters тфилин (t-f-i-l-i-n) did not forge any word that I could find in any of my Russian dictionaries. When I showed the unknown Cyrillic word to my friend Sasha, she looked, shrugged, and said, "It's *tefillin*; Jewish ornaments of some sort," leaving the problem to me.

Sasha helps.

That was not enough for me. Beyond the translator's task, I was curious. This was new learning for me, willing learning. I pick it up now decades later. My parents' first separation when I was ten years old ended my education as a Jew. But now was the time to resume. The first images I found for tefillin were very strange to me. A rabbi wearing a box, placed on his head? His arm wrapped in a black ribbon, curving around like a set of zebra's stripes. Tefillin, I learned, are also called phylacteries. I found images of beautifully engraved tefillin boxes in the catalogues of Judaica stores. I recalled the simple designs on the tefillin boxes I sketched at the Jewish Museum in Basel, having at that time no idea of their purpose nor any sense of what these boxes were intended to contain. Now here in front of me was a piece of Judaism about which I was utterly ignorant.

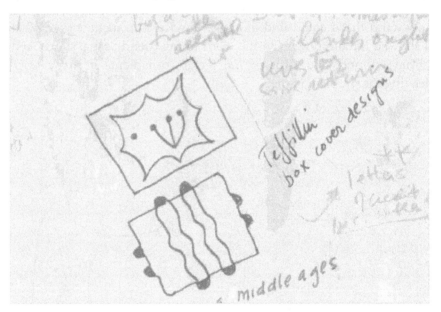

I've already mentioned how much self-learning was inherent in my process of translation: the difference in the Julian and Gregorian calendars; the different ways Europeans and Americans write a date — using different sequences for month, day, and year. And too, every now and then, the difficulties of locating a town on a map because names of cities and towns change. For example, if I were looking for Ekaterinoslav, a major city on the Dneiper south of Kiev in 1916, on a map made today, I would never find it. Why? Because today it is called Dnepropetrovsk. The important city of Proskurov, southwest of Kiev, was renamed in 1954 to Khemilnitsky (a most perfidious act of anti-Semitism in my view, wiping out Jewish history).

But now there was more than the need to get things straight in the sense of historical context and correct translation. Now there was Jewish life my family members lived and the word *tefillin* began that learning; learning of a different sort, arising from some inchoate desire. Learning I stepped back from when I, Eli and Manya's granddaughter, turned thirteen and refused to meet the rabbi for any kind of bat mitzvah process, instead hiding in the attic of my father's house until I heard the front door close after the rabbi left.

Yes, now it mattered. I wanted to know what was in the tefillin boxes—on the forehead, on the arm. Are the contents the same scriptures that are in the mezzuzahs attached in the doorway of a Jewish home? Wasn't it time I find out? Wasn't this the least I could do? What is the meaning of the Hebrew letter *shin* on the outside of the tefillin box cover? Why does the letter *shin* on these boxes sometimes have four (not three) vertical "sticks"? For that matter can I learn the meaning of the two letters, *tet* and *kaf*, that I saw on many of the Torah mantles in the Basel Museum? Endless questions. Questions I wanted to answer. I began to learn Hebrew calligraphy with master teacher Jonathan. I did lots of calligraphic homework, repeating the exercises so the calligraphy could become second hand. Gorgeous shapes and curvatures. It is a great pleasure. Maybe in some other world— future, past or lateral—I am a scribe doing just this; handwriting Hebrew texts.

I know answers to some of my questions now. I know what is inside those boxes: four scrolls. Two of the four are those that are in the mezzuzah. The two additional scrolls repeat scripture from the book of Exodus reminding us (commanding us) every year to celebrate Passover and to tell the Exodus story.

A few weeks before my own family's recent Passover (one hundred years after Manya's Passover of 1916), my nephew Nathan and I went to visit Rabbi Eli who showed us all there is to know about tefillin. He brought out two boxes—one that goes on the head, the other that goes on the arm. These two boxes, he said, were considered to be impure (a mistake in the scribe's work or incorrectly constructed) and therefore unfit for use. As a result he was able to take one of the boxes apart and show us the four scrolls inside. He also showed my nephew how to don the tefillin, wrapping his arm and hand (seven this, four that . . .), reciting prayers all along. He couldn't wrap me in the tefillin because he was an Orthodox Rabbi and therefore forbidden to touch any woman "except my wife."

I can't imagine *choosing* to wear the tefillin. Yet this Orthodox Rabbi Eli never gave me a chance to even try. I believe I would have agreed to trying it on in the privacy of the Chabad House library, even though the feeling lurked, my mother wouldn't want this. That is the sense I have. You see my mother was not a religious Jew. Not at all. My mother's father and mother had come to America from Tsarist Russia after uniting in an ardent

Rabbi Eli didn't ask me if I wanted to wear the tefillin because his orthodox views preclude this. But if he had offered, would I have said, Yes?

Wearing the tefillin.

revolutionary passion for a better world through Socialism. They were secular Jews. Activists (my grandmother as fervent as my grandfather). Revolutionaries. Socialists. *Bundists. Provocateurs.* They were members of the Jewish Labor Movement, the *Bund,* in Minsk, in what was still Tsarist Russia. They came to America not because they wanted to leave the movement to which they were tied, but on behalf of their safety.

My mother's father, my grandfather Samuel, was caught and imprisoned in 1904, along with many other Jewish *provocateurs* living in Minsk. These anti-Tsarist socialist revolutionaries were seen as fomenting trouble. After his arrest, but before sentencing, my grandfather Samuel escaped with help from his confrères and was smuggled into Europe, finally arriving in London. After a sojourn there where he learned good English, he sailed to the United States in 1906. Soon after, my grandmother Ida (*without* English) arrived in 1907. In 1908 they were registered as living in Omaha, Nebraska, continuing their political activism almost immediately. Omaha had a sufficient Jewish immigrant population with whom they immediately joined to establish a branch of the Workmen's Circle, an organization devoted to the same causes as the *Bund*. Jewish, socialist, secular, Yiddish-speaking, non-Zionist, non-international, this organization had existed in the USA for several decades. My grandfather—a handsome, tall man with a chiseled angular Romanesque face and good English—was a charismatic leader. *Two* functioning branches of the Workmen's Circle, and the construction of the Labor Lyceum in Omaha (a building for meetings and gatherings) were part of his legacy. My grandparents' connection with the Workmen's Circle—supporting the culture, welfare, and well-being of Jewish immigrants—lasted their entire lives. Both are buried at a Circle home in Medea, Pennsylvania.

Three distinctively non-religious organizations—the Workmen's Circle, the Labor Lyceum, and the Socialist party—were the loci of my mother's family life in Omaha. This was the life she breathed until she left at age 17 or so. In 1928—the year of the Presidential and gubernatorial elections—my grandfather ran on the Socialist ticket for Lieutenant Governor in the State of Nebraska alongside F. Philip Haffner, the candidate for Governor (both under Norman Thomas, America's most well-known socialist, who was running for President). My mother's parents were not religious Jews, they left that behind in Minsk forsaking religion for revolution. They were heart and soul labor advocates, socialists. Their fierce advocacy transferred to my mother (born two years after they settled in Nebraska) and never ever left her soul. Sometimes declared as radical, sometimes anarchist, sometimes called communist, my mother's family were progressives. They were for the working class, and their passion *was* firebrand. Hers too.

7. Eli Sends Money

*I*ntact and in faith, Manya's family's Passover of 1916 appears typical. The children write: *Dear Papa . . . I have a new dress* (Rivka and Ita) . . . *I have new boots* (Iosif) . . . *I have a new coat* (Niuma). Except for the fact that Eli is far away in America (*We saved a place for you at the table)*, the family is especially grateful that both Mokha and Veniamin are freed from military service. This must be the reason behind Klara's sentence in which she writes, *Our family thanks to God is living in full satisfaction. Mokha's suffering is at last over and last week he came home. For Passover the children were in nice dresses, suits . . .*

New clothes for Passover

Intact, and in faith. Eli and Manya's second oldest son Meer, keeping to the protocol established earlier to write only what can soothe and appease Eli. He writes: *I don't have much to write about myself. Each day I wear the tefillin, go to Kheder, and go to school in the fifth group. There's no more to tell about me.*

In fact it may well be, at least at this moment, it is Eli who is having the most difficulty. We can imagine this. He is apart from his wife and his six children; alone now for two years; coping with pressures to deliver money not only to Manya but to his mother, his brother and at the same time somehow save enough to buy a horse and wagon; suffering the travails of a peddler's life and occasional illness;

feeling the disconnect between expectations and realities; constantly reminding himself of the debts he owes. All combine to create a man of some misery.

For his complaints, however, he is soundly rebuked, first by his brother Meir Ben-Ami, writing in Hebrew from Palestine. Now we have a third language in our midst—Hebrew. And a third *calendric* fact: there is no exact equivalent between Hebrew and our present day calendar (unlike the exact difference of thirteen days between the Gregorian and Julian calendars). We have to simply know that the month of *Elul* roughly corresponds to the month of August/September and *Kislev* to the months of November/December.

From Eli's brother Meir Ben-Ami in Eretz Yisrael, Palestine

1916 Kislev 28

> *My dear Elijah,*
>
> *Your letter dated 18 Elul I received yesterday, the 27 of Kislev, that means three and one half months from the date it was written. Hard to describe but my happiness was beyond description. My sad and bitter thoughts passed away like a shadow. You are alive and well, and the hope to be by you and be reconnected with my brothers and sisters who live in Russia returned to me again. And the letter itself, how pleasing it was! In spite of it all, in this desperate time, you are earning more than twice as much as you were earning last year. Instead of 3-4 dollars a week last year you are now earning 8-10 dollars a week.*
>
> *But I was saddened when you spoke of your desire to return to Russia. Is it not due to your yearning to your home? Or is it because life in America does not please you? I do not understand at all how a Jew who lives in the land of light and freedom, in a land where the Jews of that land have great influence, in a land that its government breaks a treaty with cursed Russia (Oh how happy I am in its downfall). . . . How can a Jew yearn for a life of shame and humiliation in Russia full of shame and hooliganism? Has not your dwelling in the land of the free removed from your heart all*

remnants of slavery? Are you, my brother, to be likened to the slave that says "I love etc and I do not wish to be free?" In summary to earn 10 dollars a week, in a truly free land as in America and to yearn when all is said to life of slavery and degradation — all this is of great surprise to me. . . .

Klara, Manya's sister, also rebukes Eli for his complaints. In May 1916, she writes:

Greetings dear Eliyah,

. . . We were terribly upset about your health, about which you have written us twice. I will not give you any advice, do what you must to get better and God grant you a speedy recovery. I would never ask you to write Manya such an undisciplined letter [about your health problems]. After all, this kind of letter you wrote causes her great suffering. She could well lose all her strength were she to receive another such letter.

If you were in Cherkassy or in Smela, then someone could go visit you, or within two or three days get a letter from you about the condition of your health, but you are in America and we are in Russia and given the present, irregular communications one might well go out of one's mind waiting for an answer. Of course you have a need to share with someone close to you about all your sufferings and happenings, but if you knew and could see how Manya suffers, you would never write of such things so freely.

Unwillingly we are making the comparison between you and us. Really, over the last two years we have lived through very much, so much I couldn't really get it on paper. The current situation, current events, the high inflation rate, illness. We have kept this to ourselves and have not written this to you. After all this would only increase your suffering and, anyway, you can not help.

Besides, what's happening around us affects us. Mama is already sick with viral pneumonia. Veniamin has an ulcer and was near death, then he fell ill while in the military in Cherkassy with Typhoid Fever and lay in the hospital two months. Mokha has also been unwell.

As it happened I was visiting Veniamin in Cherkassy when his wife Liuba fell ill on the second day of Passover with paratyphoid. Only yesterday has she gotten up from her bed. This goes on and on but thanks to God all turned out okay. This week Veniamin goes on commission and God knows what will be with him.

God seems to look after Mokha (although with him there is much rigmarole). In Gorodische there is no good news.

Isor doesn't rebuke. He shows great compassion for his father:

Dear Papa,

I still am working with Rozenblit. He added 10 rubles to my monthly salary. . . . Dear Papa, I ask you not to give out too much credit to your customers. Try to get at least some down payment. I certainly understand that giving credit is part of trading. Just as having change is part of trading, but still you can give out too much credit and the more you have out in credit the less money you have for buying more goods.

Don't worry about us; resign yourself to your present state. I feel that sometimes you fall into despair or depressing thoughts about your situation so far from us. But I ask you to resign yourself to this fate and don't begrudge God. Of course sometimes we have to suffer. But I can write you that many people would consider themselves very fortunate if they were in your place. So many folks envy you, my God!

In the letter from Isor, there seems to be a clue as to Eli's lack of business sense. Borrowing money to buy items housewives want only to sell these on promises to pay from them leaves Eli on risky ground with debts he owes and debts owed to him. Still, the pressures from the family on Eli don't let up. Liev, Manya's father, writes: *Expenses are very high and we only receive 3/4 of what we need.* And Manya's appeals are constant: *The money that you write you are sending is very good, because I already have none. Only the salary of Isor.*

8. Making Ends Meet

*W*hy *were* prices for Manya's family's needs rising so greatly and so quickly? What happened? Russia entered World War I with the largest army in the world, 1.4 million soldiers. By war's end that figure had grown to 5 million. Yet, the Tsar's Imperial Treasury had nowhere near that amount of money to pay, supply, and arm, these soldiers. Taxes and monies borrowed from foreign governments were far from sufficient to cover the costs of war. As the first year of war turned into a second year, with no alternatives, in a desperate situation, hoping the war wouldn't last long, the Imperial Treasury printed money.

And here's what happened as a consequence. Let's take the case of the soldiers. Soldiers received rubles (printed by the Imperial Treasury in the many millions). They gave what they got to their families. That extra money would be very helpful if there were plenty of goods around that extra money could buy. But there were very few goods to buy. Take shoes, a basic item for Manya's children. When all the leather and glue and other material that go into making a shoe now went to the military to make soldiers' boots, materials for making civilian shoes became very scarce. The procurers for the war effort *took* everything they could first. Then, with newly printed money, they moved to first in line to buy what they couldn't requisition. So when Manya wanted to buy her son Meer a new pair of boots because shoes and boots *do* wear out, and children's feet grow, all the money in the world couldn't find a pair of shoes. And if by chance a merchant came across some boots and put them up for sale, immediately these pairs became subject to an auction. A guy happens to see a merchant selling boots, he runs up to the merchant, shoves a prospective buyer aside, pulls out his wallet and says, "I'll pay fifty percent *more* than what *that* guy has offered." And then another guy comes up, shoves *both* of them aside and says, "I'll pay double!" Remember, rubles they had, it's the boots that were so scarce.

Manya complained about the increasing price of a bag of flour. It's a similar story. The military requisitioned what it needed. It also enlisted peasant recruits—peasants who ordinarily would have been planting grain. The granaries became empty because the peasant was not at work in the fields but at war in the ranks of his fellow soldiers. Without grain, there was no flour. So supplies were very scarce. No wonder the prices of a family's needs are increasing. No wonder the stark figures—three four, five, six times.

The price of flour

One way for folks to cope with this inflation was to have access to dollars. And then sell those dollars on the black market at the rates many times more than what was being offered for them at the official banks. If Manya had gotten dollars from Eli she might have had enough to pay for her expenses. But Manya wasn't getting the dollars from Eli, she got rubles *at the official exchange rate* of three or four rubles to the dollar. At that rate, the dollars Eli handed over to the exchange rate employee in Philadelphia couldn't keep up with the price inflation Manya was experiencing.

It's that fast, that dramatic, and yes, I *don't* think Eli got it. If he could have participated in the black market for dollars he would have known that the dollar could get much more than what he was getting at the official exchange rate. Put another way, the exchange merchant took his dollars; Manya didn't get them, she got rubles. If she could have gotten the dollars directly (some trusted traveler taking them with him in a secret pocket, at some risk of being caught), she could have traded those dollars for many more rubles than what she was officially sent (also at some risk).

I am in a hotel room. It is 1990. I had offered to take my father with me when I next was on a business trip to Moscow. A trip he was eager to take, for his 80th birthday. One city I knew we would be visiting was Nizhny Novgorod, an historic city where the Okha and Volga Rivers converge. Each night at that hotel I would get a knock on my door. A young couple would ask, would I be willing to sell them dollars? They were offering many more rubles for my dollar than I could get with any bank. Just prior to the collapse of the Soviet Union, the instability –social, economic, financial—was rife, and the divergence between the black market rate of exchange and the official rate of exchange between dollars and rubles was stark evidence.

This kind of inflation had to have been hard—if not impossible— for Eli to imagine. First, prices in America were not changing in this way, not at all. He had no experience with such inflation. How could he understand what Manya was trying to tell him over and over. In fact in one letter from Manya in response to Eli's request to be *more* thrifty, she writes *Do you think I go to the theatre?* The whole family was trying to tell him: sending forty rubles, or even one hundred rubles, on an irregular basis was not enough. The disconnect was immense.

Manya needs not forty rubles but 100 rubles, writes Liev in December 1915.

Manya writes: *Each month we are behind. You say I should buy boots for Meer at 2.5 rubles, but I just paid the shoemaker 17 rubles!*

Klara too: *Even 100 rubles plus Isor's salary doesn't suffice.*

Eli didn't seem to get it or, he simply couldn't meet their requests. He was buying foreign currency not only for Manya but for other members of his family (his mother, his captured brother Chaim in Germany). He even offered to help his brother Meir Ben-Ami in Palestine. Nonetheless he did increase his overseas money orders to an equivalent of 100 rubles at a time from the 40 rubles he had been sending in 1915. His intentions evidently were to send 100 rubles every month. Whether he has paid more for the 100 rubles, or whether the official dollar/ruble exchange rate (how many rubles he gets to buy for the dollars he "sells") has inched up (in keeping with the reality of the situation, I am not sure). Still, Manya tries to explain. No matter what. It isn't enough.

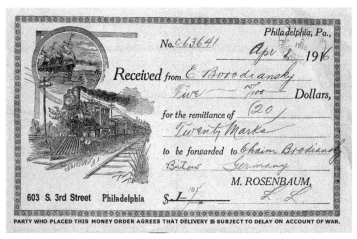

Eli's money order to Chaim, 1915

Notice of delivery of Eli's money order

Despite their urgent requests, Eli didn't have much flexibility in the matter. His wages limit the amount of dollars he has to buy rubles. The fixed exchange rates limit what they receive. Even as his earnings increase year by year, and the official fixed exchange rate inches up to (from $1=3 rubles in 1915 to $1=5.5 rubles in 1917), this could not match the increase in prices the family was experiencing.

This inflationary spiral did not end. Not until World War I, the Bolshevik Revolution, and the Civil War ended, and only after the USSR was fully established. In 1922 Eli's niece who lives in Moscow writes to Eli, *Hurrah! a long-awaited package has arrived for Manya. To get it out of customs it will be necessary to pay three million rubles.* Can you see the effect of printing money on prices which by 1921-1922 rose to such absurd amounts.

We might think the impact of a broken economy, of a nation at war on a household isn't enough to break our hearts. After all, it's only funny numbers. But not for the seven-year old boy Niuma who sees the tears flowing from his mother's eyes as she pens a letter begging once again that her husband send more money: *I need money to pay for a ration of salo* [animal fat, suet]. *It costs 40 rubles.* Then two weeks later: *I am most worried. I have neither letter nor money from you in five weeks. I am frying with rationed salo and spilling tears.* Yes, it can break a little heart. No wonder then that when it is his turn to write a line, Niuma writes *Papa. Come Home. I do not want to go to America. I want you to come home.*

9. My Parents Separate, Reconcile, Divorce

I do not know if my mother knew about my father's affections for other women. Of course she must have. But even if so, even if she had, I am guessing, she still might well have wanted to keep her family together. She did finally have a good paying job at National Institutes of Health in Bethesda. She could have managed financially I believe. She *was* managing financially I think. But my father's company required him to transfer to New York City. He asked my mother for a reconciliation. This had to have been difficult. But she caved.

I am guessing she was feeling guilt at having us kids come home from school with no one there, feeling guilt when her plan for after-school care failed. The caretakers she found (who would live with us rent free but be at home for us after school) were the caretakers all three of us kids hated and so she ended that arrangement quickly. My sister was now a rebellious teenager, and when we would come back from wherever we had been and see the house dark to find my sister and her boyfriend also there in the dark, my guess is her will weakened. Perhaps she knew of suggestions of her unacceptable life style in those days — a father separate. I do not know. I cannot say. Did she still love him? Was it delusional hope?

Their reconciliation and subsequent move to Ridgewood, New Jersey seemed to bring my mother new excitement. She must have believed that their renewed commitment to each other was genuine on the part of my father and would be lasting. That not working would open up new opportunities for her. I don't know. I only know that instead of finding a paying job suitable for her, she threw her energies into putting together, organizing, founding a Jewish Youth Club as part of the local Jewish Community Center (JCC). I remember her urgency that I participate. I can't say exactly what motivated her. She didn't need paid work because my father's salary was now sufficient? So, instead, she could put to work her deep beliefs held fast from her parents, *for Jewish social organization beyond religious training*. She threw her whole self into this volunteer work, gaining great appreciation. "You have accomplished so much in such an intelligent, dignified, and efficient manner, and with such devotion as to put most of us to shame" wrote M. Weinberg, presiding officer of the JCC, in a letter to her.

Regardless of religious intent, she wrote in a proposal she submitted for approval by the board of the JCC, *the aims of the Youth Club were: (1) To develop our potentials as democratic social beings; (2) find opportunities for making friendships with our own kind; (3) understand some of the problems facing the American Jew and (4) strengthen our reverence for the poetry, spiritual values and wisdom found in the Jewish heritage.* Certainly the priorities were those of her parents, and firmly held in her soul: a zeal for a better world.

My mother tried to get me to become active in that Jewish teen club during those two years we lived in New Jersey. That didn't work for me. I don't remember anything about the club's activities, only my mother pressuring me to give a speech before the larger congregation about something or other. No, I wasn't involved in any real way. Rather, as a pre-pubescent teen, I was obsessed with the fact that I was the least popular girl in my eighth-grade class (of course, I was new!); obsessed by the fact that during a field trip with five girls packed in the back seat of a car, someone raised my blouse and said, *Look, Elisa has no breasts!*

I have almost no recollection of my father being part of our life in Ridgewood, New Jersey. I believe he stayed nights in New York "for work." But my mother seemed content with a garden and her volunteer work. Yet, there was a cost of this volunteer work for her. Just a short year after her efforts in New Jersey were bearing fruit, another action of my father's company meant a move to Connecticut if we were going to stay together. There was no talk of him giving up his job to look for another and therefore negate the reason to move. His company's new headquarters were now in New London, CT close to the Rhode Island border. Neither of my parents expected this, but it was my mother for whom the consequences were grave. Having had no employment work in Ridgewood, having spent her time instead volunteering for a cause she believed in, she wasn't prepared financially to even consider staying in town with her children on her own, without an employed spouse. Despite the separation in Bethesda where she was fully employed, fully rewarded, and holding her own financially, in Ridgewood New Jersey this was inconceivable. She didn't have any work experience in this town. So, now at 47, she moved to an utterly unfamiliar rural environment in Eastern Connecticut, with a man who at some point during that time she learned was involved with a certain Mary Steuteville. This brought her down.

Mary was to become my step-mother just a short few years later. They were married less than nine months after my parents' final split and just a few months after the final divorce decree. My father had met and courted Mary during the three years my mother was working in Bethesda when my father had lived separately in a D.C. apartment. He reconciled with my mother nonetheless when his career path necessitated the move to the New York area. He couldn't have been honest with my mother. I doubt he was interested in understanding my mother. She wanted to use her passion and her intelligence beyond that used for raising children. She *needed* to use her passion and intelligence. My father was indifferent to that. An artiste, talented, used to philandering. Very busy and focused at his work. Successful and upwardly mobile. His creativity seemed paramount. He had to have been spoiled. As the youngest of six children growing up in Gorodische, he was always being praised for his special talents (*He is so clever. At five, he writes Jewish and Russian! He draws so well.*)

No, I do not believe my father was interested in understanding my mother. I do believe however that he was interested (*surely, he was interested, wasn't he?*) in his children and keeping a family together. And so we moved from New Jersey to Connecticut. There, my father's first steps in our new world in Old Saybrook, Connecticut was to participate actively in *his* version of Jewish life—joining a synagogue nearby and moving quickly into a leadership role. Now it was my father who tried to encourage me to engage in a Jewish life and go with him to Friday night services at Temple located in Moodus, a few towns away. I, however, was as indifferent as my mother was. Jewish *religious practice* was as foreign to my mother as her Jewish *revolutionary politics* was to my father. But that was beside the point for me. Old Saybrook, the town we were living in, and the high school I was attending seemed to have no Jews. I had no incentive to identify myself as different, or to be Jewish. I wanted to fit in. I had made friends. I wanted to belong. I was honing new skills—skills of liking everyone, belonging to no one group, crossing between groups—skills that were serving me well. A leader in various school activities, my classmates voted me to be chair of our Junior Prom. Yet, at the same time, no one asked me to go to this Prom and my father's flower corsage he had purchased for me to wear sat in the refrigerator alone that night.

Yes there was something positive, good, and real between me and my father despite *their* troubles. It centered around a bond we were building regarding my creative school work. Sometime during my "growing up" years I realized my father understood my creativity and accepted it. The moment of discovery happened one afternoon. We were kneeling on the floor in front of a large two by three feet posterboard, drawing an entry for a poster contest sponsored by the National Forest Service's Prevention of Forest Fires Programme. I may have been in fifth or sixth grade. I don't remember winning any prize, and really it was my father's hand rather than mine in the drawing we made but we got the perfect image and caption for the space and yes, my soul rejoiced. The image occupying the whole space was a simple match stick. The two-line caption read: *Friend if you're careful. Foe if you're not.* Both of us knew we had succeeded, both of us felt the satisfaction.

My father and I took a walk one fall day during my junior year in high school when we were living in Old Saybrook. We talked mostly about a paper I was writing for a homework assignment about an old grist mill. Drawing, sign making, calligraphy, now writing, joined our shared conversations. I felt a tug toward my father. Maybe he felt a tug toward me as well. In this creative sense we were pals, that much I knew. I knew he knew I wanted these efforts of mine to be satisfying, creatively and emotionally. That this mattered to me a lot. Perhaps even more than belonging in the small town where I had been planted.

Did I belong? Could I ever have belonged? How can we know these things? Did I try to belong but it didn't work? Did it not work because I was a Jew in a gentile world?

During a one week course as a selected delegate to the national program, Girls State/Boys State, I did find "puppy love" with Steve Knup, also a delegate, from a very Catholic family. This relationship was short-lived because before my senior year, my parents had started divorce proceedings, and my mother, brother and I moved to Boston. I was sixteen.

The move from suburban New Jersey to Old Saybrook in rural eastern Connecticut had to have been difficult for my mother. It was there, having to start again to find a purpose, a life worth living, where my mother flagged. Locked her bedroom door literally and succumbed. Whatever it was between mother and father—a recent letter she found from my father's "old flame" Mary, or, "scythe against stone" as my father said—these matters finally took their toll.

The problem is that my mother had left New Jersey on some basis of trust, or on some belief that my father and she could still have a lasting partnership. She left behind engaging volunteer work effort to move to rural Connecticut where then she found out about my father's (continuing) attraction to Mary. This was like a sledge hammer crushing any hopes of conjugal life. She was in a desert, her desires slammed, compacted. She was facing a life without form, foundation, fulfillment. *Of course I am who I am.* I now say. *Of course I would never want to be like my mother.* In a last desperate act before the start of my senior year she gathered my younger brother and me and a few suitcases, hired a taxi to take us to the railroad station, rented a basement apartment in Brookline, a suburb of Boston, and initiated the process of suing my father for divorce. I have to assume my mother was hoping for a better life for herself. It never happened. Instead, a rotten divorce settlement followed by a series of secretarial jobs without meaning or challenge. Depression. Loneliness. Poverty.

We children tried to help. We wanted so much more for her. We knew her need for learning. The intense pleasure she derived from learning. None of us have forgotten the wafts of satisfaction that she sent our way as she got so deeply involved writing a paper about Thomas Paine during a course she took from somewhere at some point. Like wafts from a master's culinary kitchen. Pleasing, delicious. We were unified in our goal to help her fund a college degree. She applied for and was accepted in a special program for older, working adults at Goddard College. Goddard College awarded her the BA degree, her advisor calling the paper she wrote (*Creative Dramatics for a Human Centered Curriculum*) brilliant . . . useful, innovative." But it was too late. She was already 57 years old. She never found a suitable job. She wandered from Boston to New London, Connecticut where my sister lived, then to Florida where one of her sisters lived, then to Santa Cruz where another one of her sisters lived, then to Seattle. To me.

10. Meer Joins the Red Army

There are no letters after December 31, 1917. We can begin to see why. The Tsarist state has collapsed. The capitol of Russia, Petrograd (soon to be renamed Leningrad), has changed hands in the name of a Socialist Revolution. But Civil War was brewing. Who would fill the vacuum left by the Tsarist collapse? Who would consolidate rule? The city of Kiev, the province of Kiev, all the southwestern provinces of former Imperial Russia on both sides of the Dnieper River now became open territory, up for grabs: by Polish neighbors, by Ukrainian Independence fighters, by Cossack armies, and by the Bolsheviks. The chaos was military, political, and economic. The old order has collapsed, fully gone. Yet lots of armed soldiers and officers, as well as armed peasants, were roaming about. All unreliable, fickle, with uncertain and disparate agendas and finally too weak to stave off the Bolsheviks and Trotsky's Red Army. It takes the Bolshevik partisans, the Communist Party and the Red Army three years of civil war and even a war with Poland to consolidate authority. Until then no authority was in place long enough to enable normal public activities to resume.

So there is a blackout on my sources: No Manya, no Mokha, no Isor to help me (*much less to help Eli)* know what is happening. Three years of silence: 1918, 1919, and 1920. "We are cut off from the world: neither railroads, nor mail, nor telegraphs nor telephones. Everything is grapevine news," writes a diarist in the Fall of 1918. "Nothing functions."

Of course nothing functioned. Consider this: besides the collapse of the Tsarist State and the socialist revolutions of February and October 1917, Russia's war with the German and Austro-Hungarian Empires (on Russia's Western Front) had still to come to a close. That would take almost all of 1918. Meanwhile German and Austro-Hungarian armies, though planning for withdrawals, are *still in the same positions as when hostilities were ongoing. And the armies still armed*. World War I will soon be over, but in our theatre, war itself was anything but over. Immediately, latent and new impulses arose. To repeat, lots of loose armed soldiers with their various commanders looking to their various agendas; separate, agendas, unpredictable and chaotic. The factions are many: the Bolsheviks, the revanchists, the monarchists, the army for Ukrainian National Independence, peasant militarists and, finally, the "crazies"—death-defying Cossack bands, anarchists, or simply hoodlums out for a rout.

How am I going to fill in this blackout? I want to understand, so I research, read, and map. I especially take to the maps because I am trying to relate all to our center point, Gorodische. I want to feel Manya's world. Imagining what my grandmother was going through is not possible, but I could try to understand the latent and new impulses that drove the region, her world and, ultimately, her family into chaos.

There were the events: battles, armies, uprisings, turnabouts, betrayals, banner-led politics, changing alliances. There were the military egos: commanders named Makhno, Grigoriev, Petliura, Denikin, Wrangle and others. There were the soldiers: wary, hungry, sodden, besotted. There were the peasants: revengeful, armed, against all authority. There was the breakdown of infrastructure creating a blackout (*All is grapevine.*) There were the towns, the villages, the country estates, places where theft, murder, rape, total destruction happened. And there was Gorodische.

Let's see what the letters tell us from the summer of 1916 to the end of 1917 before the blackout began. One family matter seems to be Meer. Manya writes to Eli: *It seems from your letters you think our son Meer is cooperating, that he is in agreement with us. No. He talks to me as if I am a ten-year old. "I do not want to be a salesman," he says. I don't know what to do about him. I don't do well without you in this regard. "OK," I say to him, "then what are you going to do?" He doesn't answer.* Klara too writes, *Meer is very unhappy with your advice that he work as a salesman. He very much wants to be learning but evidently not in the sense of learning to earn money for the family.*

Inexplicably, there is a gap in the cache of letters from Gorodische, an eight-month hiatus from August 1916 until Isor writes in April 1917 a short few sentences about the February Revolution, the Kerensky Provisional Government, and the fallen Tsarist monarchy.

Isor writes:

Nothing new with us except that which is new for everyone—you see we are now free citizens. All national boundaries are changed. But in a word, really, nothing is very different. Today in Gorodische was a big demonstration and much singing. In a word all of Russia is now celebrating its Easter/its Passover/its Freedom. It remains to want only that the war will end which seems to be coming.

Manya writes not a word about these events. Throughout the summer to the end of 1917 Manya writes many letters and postcards to Eli. The subjects are the same: the awful length of time between letters and the dire need for money. She writes in August 1917: *You say you are sending 500 rubles for five months. You say 100 rubles should last for one month. It doesn't.* In December 1917, she writes: [I spent] *100 rubles for one bag of flour.* Manya is silent about the political events surrounding their lives, but her anxieties are everywhere evident. *I am so worried and agitated I don't know how I can live—is it that you don't write or it is something else? I received a postcard from you about three weeks ago dated the first of February and I haven't received any money in a long time. Without money, it's bad.*

Take note Manya is writing on the 28th of May about a letter she received from Eli dated the first of February. That means the transit time was almost four months.

The breakdown seemed to be both directions. Some of Eli's letters surely did not get to Manya at all, or are months late. Similarly, some letters *from* Gorodische also took months to arrive. We know this from the envelope markings which show both the date posted in Gorodische and the date of arrival in Wilmington Delaware. It is curious however that money does arrive from Eli in June.

Eli gets a glimpse from the words of Meer and Isor about the changes since the February Revolution. From Meer: *Dear Papa. Here in Gorodische I built a library of which I am chairperson. Don't think it is a library, it is a place where everyone studies and it has a kindergarten where I work. Also there is now a theatre group where I also spend time.*

Isor also writes about the changes: *The Department Store, SPEKTOR, has liquidated its assets. All the workers are paid off, the amounts according to a formula worked out by the professional society of workers now free. Grandfather will receive 6000 to 7000 rubles.*

The Socialists were recreating property definitions away from private/for profit to communal/for all. Eli in Wilmington was learning about this all from afar and no doubt was in a state of ignorance, uncertainty and worry. Knowing from the newspapers about the impending strength of the Bolshevik bid to consolidate power over its other revolutionary rivals, we well expect that Eli would ask about the family coming to the USA. Isor responds in two letters, one in October, the other in December 1917.

Dear Papa,

There is much news here, practically all of life has become new in the time since your departure, but there is no possibility to write about it now. . . Now we will see whether our national anthem will be proven true. Only God knows what He is doing. He doesn't punish for nothing. I would like to write you more about this but it isn't possible. We'll save for a better time all the stories about our separated lives.

Papa! I just received your postcard dated 23 September. To answer your question I can say that the subject—Can we get to America?—is a very large question in general and even larger during this present time. Nowadays there can't even be a mention of leaving. It will be necessary to endure still our separation. Dearest Papa! Have patience. We are okay. For heaven's sake! Be well, don't worry. Try not to give out too much credit. Grandpa will write another time. Right now he doesn't have the mood/spirit to write.

In fact, Liev, Manya's father, never writes again. He dies a year later. Isor again:

Dear Papa,

It seems you are most concerned about the most serious question of where shall we live? You ask us in your letters what is our opinion, our desires, but believe me we ourselves don't know how to answer you. Buying some property here in these times isn't possible. First of all, because of the high rate of inflation, which you can't imagine; secondly the present situation doesn't allow the buyer any kind of freedom to buy. The situation in Russia right now is such that in general one cannot say anything with certainty.

Probably you aren't informed very well about the turmoil here. God only knows what form the revolution here will take, what it will look like. Now Russia is undergoing changing times; what will result? There is no way to know. So in view of that to say anything in the present time about leaving or staying in Russia is very difficult. The question then under present circumstances must remain unanswered.

Personally, I would prefer to live in Russia, however again, I do not know what kind of revolution will overtake matters here, and if necessary I will go to America. Little by little life will return to normal, then the question of where to live will be able to be decided. For now everything with us is okay.

Isor

Klara (Manya's sister) attaches a note, written in her more emotional style:

Dear Eliyah:

Today we received a postcard from you in which you express the desire that Manya and the children go to you. I am surprised that you can suddenly decide such a question during these moments. I don't think anyone would risk their lives during these times and I don't know whether anyone is leaving. No one can picture what's ahead. Of course we want that your family join you; especially strong feelings are with your eldest daughter and my sister (your wife) who has been "dreaming" about this for a very long time. Despite all that is happening I believe and I hope that we will see each other in full health and in good manner despite our horrible situation right now.

Manya has enormous expenses and generally what is happening with us would not be possible for you to imagine. . . . Will our

70

suffering end soon? Ah, Eliyah, will we ever be able to forget (bury)
this madness and can we endure these terrible tensions?

Postcards sent in November 1917 show stamped dates of arrival in Wilmington Delaware of *four to five months later*. The postcard stamped November 10, 1917 leaving Gorodische shows its date of arrival in the USA March 25, 1918. Postal communications have broken down. Despite Eli's questions to Manya about his family leaving Russia for America, reunion seems further away than ever. The gates were closing. At year's end we know (from family history) that Mokha joined the Communist Party. We know Meer joined the Red Army. We know that Isor stayed put as Manya's head of household.

That's all we know as the curtains close.

Despite my father's humorous essay (written much later in America and included below) about deposing the Tsar, the rabbi, and all things troubling at age seven, I can imagine a small boy swirling about, very unsteady in the tumultuous revolutionary winds that followed the 1917 revolutions. Remember he was the youngest, closest to his mother, very present to her anxieties. He had to say goodbye to his beloved brother Meer (a soul mate in the artistic sense) who joined the Red Army and who he never saw again. He is present to the eclipse of his grandfather's prestige as the private sector fell to the socialist programme. His Uncle Mokha, now a Communist Party official, is increasingly busy and absent. Isor too is traveling wherever he could for whatever he could to support his mother and his siblings. This is the chaos of government collapse, revolution, civil war. No wonder, he writes: *Papa! Come Home!*

From the Papers of Benjamin P. Brodinsky (Niuma)

DEPOSING THE CZAR AND THE REBBE

I became a revolutionary at age five.

My first task was to get rid of Czar Nicholas the Second, whose picture I used to see in the police station and who called himself, strangely, I thought, "We, the Emperor . . . ."

My work as a revolutionary was carried on in secrecy at first. I listened carefully to what my uncles and aunts were saying and I saw that they were right. The czar had to go. Then I became expert at making fun of him and orating, "We, the Czar of all the Russias . . . ." This used to make everyone laugh and they asked me to repeat my mimicry whenever we were alone in the house and there was no danger of outsiders coming in. I also joined in singing little ditties about the nasty Czarina, Rasputin, and the little Czareviches who lived in a big palace and ate from golden dishes, while we starved.

My revolutionary work helped, because one morning I learned the Romanoffs — the whole kit and caboodle — were gone.

My next tasks were to make certain the counterrevolutionary forces of Denikin, Wrangle and Petliura (what nasty White Russian generals they were!) were defeated; and then to see to it that Lenin and Trotsky were safe and took control of the government.

Finally, it was part of my revolutionary program to banish the cheder-rabbi from our town so that would he would never again grab my ear, fling me into a corner and order me to memorize the Shema, the Kiddush and more than a dozen blessings over food, new clothing, on seeing the rainbow, on smelling a flower for the first time in the spring—and God knows what else.

I also had a quarrel with God, but I hesitated to include Him in my revolutionary program because I wasn't sure I could best Him.

So the rebbe and the cheder became my immediate targets. I was four when my mother made an arrangement with Reb Mortke to take me on as a pupil. She saw to it that I attended that cheder every day, regardless of the weather, the muck and mire on the streets after the rains, or the darkness on winter afternoons.

The cheder (the word means room) was dark and smelled of old prayer books, mixed with the smell of cabbage the rebbe's wife was cooking in the kitchen. Most of the room was taken by a very long wooden table, with hard long benches placed around it. When I arrived, I took a seat at one end of the table and joined boys of my age in reciting out loud the alef bet and combinations of vowels and consonants. All day long our voices chanted: bo, ba, be, boo; do da, de, doo, mo, ma, me , moo .

While making these sounds, I kept an eye on the older boys around the table, as they read complete Hebrew words and translated them into Yiddish. Soon, I, too, was staring into the pages of a Bible, with yellow and tattered pages, held up before me by another boy with whom I shared The Good Book. And starting with the first word, Breishis, that is, "In the beginning," I began to study the Five Books of Moses.

It was easy. All I had to do was read a word in Hebrew, wait until the rebbe translated it for me in Yiddish, and then sing out both the Hebrew and Yiddish words. When I got to be five or six, I began to work my way through long prayers to be said in the synagogue on weekdays, Sabbath and Holidays. At the same time, I had to memorize a host of blessings to be said when eating bread, drinking water, when biting into an apple, when it thundered, when lightning flashed, and when encountering a dead dog in the street. Of the blessings to be stuffed into my head there seemed no end—and they hastened the final and decisive conflict between me, Rebbe Mortke and God.

The rebbe, as I remember him, wore a long, black tunic, a yarmulke on his head, and carried a short, slender rod to which three or four even shorter leather tongs had been lashed at one end. He never used the switch on a pupil. He used to whip the table, or the side of a bench, when a boy displeased him. He never sat down. He roamed about the room, circling the table, shouting orders, correcting mistakes, yanking up now one child after another. When his anger arose against a boy, he would put down the switch at the head of the table, where The Good Book rested, move slowly toward his victim, look at him carefully, pause, as if deciding whether to slap the boy's face or pull his ear. These were his favorite means of punishment, often capped by banishment into a corner for an hour.

He liked me. I was small and looked frail at age six. I could read words he had never taught me, having learned them at home from my older brothers. He would praise me by saying, "That's right, that's right."

Then it happened—on a dark, gloomy winter day. We had just finished an account of the death of Moses, in Deuteronomy. My eyes were full of tears. But the rebbe immediately ordered the younger boys to recite a string of blessings. He ordered me to recite the blessing to be said when encountering a funeral procession. I stammered, then stopped. The rebbe's face darkened. His eyes grew large with menace. He moved toward me.

"You heathen with a wooden heart," he cried, grabbed me by an ear and hurled me into a corner.

It was then I decided the rebbe, like the Czar, had to be deposed.

* * * * *

"No more cheder!" It was my brother Joe (Iosif) saying this and I didn't believe it. I hadn't yet made my final plans for revolt against the rebbe. But since no one in the house said anything when Joe and I spent the morning playing marbles outdoors instead of going to cheder, I accepted Joe's words.

Why cheder came to a sudden end, I didn't try to determine. I gave it a thought or two —Did the rebbe die? Did Mother run out of money for my tuition? I also reasoned that my uncles and aunts, knowing the Revolution would soon break into the open, had convinced my mother that the cheder had to go the way of the Imperial Autocracy, and the rebbe, the way of Nicholas the Second, Ruler of all the Russias. I didn't ask any questions.

* * * * *

* * * * *

9 Nov 1917 front
9 Nov 1917 back

NOTE: If you look carefully at the postmarks, you will see that the postcard was mailed from Gorodische on November 10, 1917 and arrived in New York on March 25, 1918–a total of more than four months.

75

11. My Marriage, My Divorce

*A*fter the taxi ride to the train and the train to Boston, I spent my senior year in a new high school, Brookline High. This high school was full of Jewish kids. I didn't have to have this outsider life anymore. But something had happened by then. I can state with fair accuracy I was taking on the closed-down-ness of my mother. This divorce wasn't working out for her and it wasn't working for me either.

I had one friend during my senior year, Gisela Lenz, a refugee from the Hungarian Revolution of 1956. Even though Brookline High was full of Jews, I had no social life other than walking to and from school with Gisela. Her trauma so near to her that one day she was appalled that I had picked my fingernail to the point of blood. "Blood everywhere," she said. "The Danube river was full of blood." After the school day I worked at one of the oldest and most elite country clubs in America: *The Country Club*. For the Boston Brahmin, I was told. I was a waitress for the dinner hour and on weekends. I remember black limousines driving past me as I walked up the long driveway in the cold winter, up from a bus stop.

I did attract one guy during that year in Brookline, a red-headed Irish fellow, Ernie Carmichael. He liked me in so far as he could steal shirts from a small clothing store right across the street then duck into our apartment. This way, no one was able to track him down. I agreed to a blind date for my senior prom. My mother's friend helped me to buy a dress. I was shy, afraid, and miserable the whole night.

My Mom was a mess. I was a mess. The bum divorce settlement had started her downward spiral. I had only one year living with her and my brother before I would be off to college, but that year was excruciatingly painful for me. She and I shared a bedroom, my brother slept on the living room couch. With her dresser light still on, I would lay in my bed reading or writing letters to the boyfriend I had met during the Boys State/Girls State convention, while she picked at her face in a magnifying mirror. Night after night after night until I fell asleep. These one-bedroom apartments were all she could afford. During the one year, we moved once or twice—always to something worse, like dark basements. But it wasn't the relative poverty of our life, it was the poverty of emotional strength. She didn't have it and couldn't give it to me.

Just as I repressed my openness to experiencing life, I repressed my Jewish identity. As a child, during Sunday School, I often played the role of Queen Esther during our Spring holiday of Purim. The story of Purim features a beautiful Jewish girl, chosen to be Queen of Persia, who intervened, at her peril, to influence her husband, the anti-Semite King, to save her people, the Jewish people, who were under threat of annihilation by the King's evil advisors. Esther is beautiful in appearance, spirit and soul. And courageous. My role at Sunday School was the preferred role—Queen Esther who, my father would emphasize, always won the beauty contest. Yet, the storms of my parents' troubles had torn away my power as a Queen Esther. The peripatetics of my parents' unhappy marriage, separations of one kind or another (two beds, separate bedrooms, living apart, a locked bedroom, divorce) had taken its toll on me. My Jewish persona was over.

Not that both parents didn't try as I have said. But it was too late. The poison of a toxic marriage had rifled my soul. Matter had been sucked out.

That senior year in High School was very lonely. My father didn't come to my graduation. He was in Chicago at his wedding with Mary. My feminine power nil. I had become shy in the presence of guys. I considered myself unattractive. I began to want to hide. Small breasted, how could I flout myself anywhere, to anyone. A separateness, a feeling I was unattractive to others. Dark skinned with faint hair on my upper lip. And yet, at the same time, I was building personal success of a different and new sort. The ability to be comfortable where others might not be. The ability to have no strong persona other than one which does not threaten others. A new behavior pattern took hold the first two years of college life at University of Connecticut before I transferred to UC Berkeley. I made friends with everyone on my floor of our all-women dorm. The women on the other floors too. I was inclusive. I didn't belong to any particular group. I joined no groups. I was available for everyone and had a genuine curiosity about everyone. This is where I was comfortable. In this manner I could enter into other people's worlds. I didn't belong to any one group.

I wasn't pigeon-holed. This strategy worked in my favor. The girls insisted I run for a student leadership position. I got the votes of all 81 girls in my dorm. The ability to be comfortable where others might not be; not to be a threat to others in unknown or uncertain situations; to welcome differences—these behaviors would serve me well years later: the move away from the east coast to California; during a two-year sojourn in America's Deep South; in the Peace Corps in Africa; during my Russia-related career.

Comfortable in unusual settings, yet shy and uncomfortable as a woman, dates were rare. The only dates I had were from other waiters in the summer hotels I worked at. One of them I lost my virginity to. Another one of them became my first husband. This was a Southern boy, a genuine rebel, who was shredding his family's hopes for him by announcing he was taking seasonal work at Yellowstone National Park, and after that permanent work as a cowboy. He had just come North as I was going West — also for summer work at Yellowstone and then on to the University of California at Berkeley for my junior year. We intersected. We kept in touch.

During a year abroad before entering graduate school at Berkeley, I lived for a summer in Croatia. Having a Slavic last name Brodinsky was acceptable in Croatia and from that point on, I wanted to learn Russian and continue my studies in economics, particularly the Russian economic system. This suited both of my parents. It suited my father for the role of languages in this course of study. It suited my mother for the prominent role of alternative economic systems. In addition, two Jewish professors of mine were very encouraging. It is their encouragement that I heard. So I studied. I had no boyfriends. But I had kept in touch with the Southern rebel. He invited me to visit him at a high mountain Colorado ranch where he had a "dream" job. Six months later he asked me to marry him. I accepted. We were different but *connecting nonetheless* in a feat of cultural and mutual accommodation or innovation like when blacks and whites marry. At least that is how I saw it. Cultural accommodation was something I had in my power to do rather well. But accepting his offer and toeing my party line of adherence to inter-cultural values meant living in a non-Jewish world; connecting to the *other* and disconnecting from myself. A separateness *forever*.

78

Was I *deliberately* agreeing to assume the persona of outsider? Despite my Jewishness, did I feel safer somehow in this kind of setting than being with my kind? Was I creating for myself, deliberately, an outsider status (a Jew in a gentile world) to allow myself the role in which I was most comfortable? Proving I can bridge cultures, explain cultural differences? Proving my power?

We lived for two years in Mississippi. I worked as a public librarian, my husband worked with anti-poverty agencies. I became pregnant with our daughter Rachael, and we joined the Peace Corps and went to Cameroun, West Africa. There a violent and irredeemable incident took place between us, and I left him. I returned to the USA with my one and one-half year old daughter to stay in the Old Saybrook house of my teenage years with my father and Mary, his wife. Yes I opted for comfort and the ease of my father's spacious home. The home my mother had left over a decade earlier. My daughter was still a toddler, I needed support and my step-mother, a kind elegant soul, and my father could provide that. Now divorced and a single-parent, I found work at nearby Yale University for a fine wage as a research economist. There I met a gentile from the Midwest temporarily teaching at Yale. After a colleague of his helped him land a job in Seattle, he asked me to marry him. I accepted. And we moved to Seattle.

Did I know I had choices? There were a few Jewish guys in my life and I did feel more relaxed with them. But I couldn't say that's what I wanted or needed. I could sense I was deserving of something I might want but didn't know what it was.

So I married another someone for whose family I would be an alien, a foreigner. I had honed that skill of being lovable to gentiles, to others, to non-Jews. I didn't hide the fact of my Jewish heritage. I was sure to host Passover every year. I just wasn't involved with Jewish folks and almost all of our Passover guests were gentiles. A separateness *forever*.

12. Reindeer in the Arctic

*H*ow did I get here? Up on the continental divide in the Arctic Circle making markets? People always asked such questions. My answer was routine. My "dutiful daughter" path led me to a niche market in academia: East-West trade. When my new husband and I (along with my two-year old daughter Rachael) landed in Seattle for his work, I got a teaching job at the University of Washington. The subject—the Russian economic system, alternatives to capitalism—for my mother; research in the Russian language for my father.

Innocent and inspired, yeo-woman, I worked, fully engaged. My research, unique and original—looking at Russia in its capacity as a player in the Pacific Rim consortium of nations—caught the eyes of my more-established colleagues. Egged on and willing, already published and having already had an opportunity for two feet on the ground in the Russian Far East, I decided to get a PhD in this same subject. As a PhD student came opportunities for research travel grants.

Innocent and inspired, each step successful, I could not stop. So after the PhD when another opportunity arose to be the first ever academic exchange researcher in the Russian Far East under a newly concluded 1988 US-USSR Bilateral Agreement, I could not but apply. The final interview in Princeton was with a professor who happened to be Jewish. That interview was easy; as if I were talking to my uncle. I got the award. I had asked for a stay of four months. I put on my shield of defense: *I can do this. Why can't I? Why shouldn't I?*

That research grant paved a foundation for my peddler work. For wasn't I doing the same work as my grandfather but two generations later? Making markets? Striving to make markets? Bringing buyers and sellers together; gathering information for entrepreneurs and capital investors? How far and wide I went! The furthest inland I went from Russia's Pacific Coast was to the Republic of Sakha, or Yakutiia, a large administrative territory in the eastern part of the Russian-dominated great Eurasian plain. Sakha encompassed the great Lena River which ran from the South to the North, emptying out in the Arctic Circle. Yakutsk, the capitol, had been (and for all I know still is) the administrative center for exiled prisoners. Agents processed prisoners there and then sent them on to various gulag mining or logging camps to the north or further to the northeast. On that singular trip I was visiting as an official guest of the Governor (a tit for tat since I had arranged for the same Governor to visit our city of Seattle for a conference on joint cooperation).

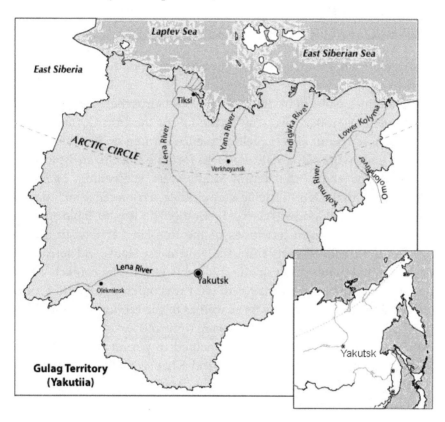

Yakutsk is the capitol of the administrative territory in which sits Verkhoyansk, the place of punishment for my maternal grandfather's revolutionary compatriots apprehended by Tsarist police in Minsk in 1905. (Of 4,526 political deportees to Siberia in January 1905, 1,676 or 37 percent were Jews.) As much as 35 to 40 percent of political deportees to Yakutiia between 1893 and 1905 were Jews. The Jewish nationality was documented on internal passports until 1997. But at that time I had no thoughts of who was sent here or how and when. My excitement was focused on the possibility of experiencing "the whisper of the

81

stars," for I was in a place where it can be so cold an exhalation of a breath turns into ice crystals.

My mother was driven. Her mother was driven. I am driven. Yes, the drive to lead a fulfilled life was ferocious in my mother and drove her to a kind of madness. Not the kind of madness that lands one in an institution in a straitjacket, but madness nonetheless; overwhelming depression, negating the ability to make reasonable choices.

I wasn't going to live her life. I was going to succeed. I was going to surpass those clumps of men, always seen at podiums around the world.

The times were right. In the late 1980s Gorbachev's glasnost and policy of perestroika gave way to the fall of the Iron Curtain on its western borders but also to melting the Ice Curtain on its easternmost border. Endeavors of the State of Alaska for state and citizen diplomacy and dialogue across the Bering Straits were succeeding. Dialogue expanded with the North Pacific Round Table, a conference included in the 1990 Summer Goodwill Games in Seattle. This Round Table brought leaders from all seven territories of the Russian Far East to Seattle to meet their counterparts from the Northwest states and territories of the United States and Canada. I led this effort. The contacts I had made during my research stay paid off: I was much in demand for the knowledge I had of the players as well as of the economic situation in that little known region. The times were right and I was right, front and center. Warming bilateral relations helped to permit Alaska Airlines to start flights between Anchorage and Khabarovsk in exchange for Aeroflot flights along the same route. Again, I was involved. The establishment in 1994 of the Gore-Chernomyrdin U.S.-Russian Joint Commission on Economic and Technological Cooperation gave a signal to businesses that investing in Russia just might pay off.

Yes, indeed, *I* would be the main speaker on the podium at the International Conference in Moscow on Offshore Oil and Gas Development, and it would be me who would make the case for offshore drilling in the Russian Pacific Region. Not anyone else.

And it would be because of my good research, careful analysis. Not part of any old-boy system, nor playing sexual politics. Just hard work, good work, fun work. And successful work: formed, fulfilling, finished. Hard work, continuous work. Successful work. I would never get distracted, never veer off course. Did those clumps of men usually on the podiums all by themselves know I was on occasion offered the pleasures of a young boy for the evening? Surely they would have laughed because they knew my job excluded hanky panky. It was for them to accept the offers of young women for the evening. But they knew too not to come knocking on my hotel door drunk and predatory. Traveling in Russia was particularly suited for that masculine nonsense.

An excerpt from my 1994 journal:

Yakutiya. Cold. March. The only other guests in this hotel for foreigners are two airline pilots who are flying freight charters. The city of Yakutsk feels empty as if all the inhabitants are on holiday. A small outdoor market is operating near the hotel despite the cold—minus 30 degree centrigrade. Vendors, bundled in various sets of bulky jackets all with big hoods up or with Russian fur hats flaps down, huddle near open grills. They are selling hot food from the grill and a variety of boxed and canned grocery items as well as crates of impoverished cabbages, carrots and potatoes. The day is gray and it feels like dusk is coming on. Customers are few and I figure the market will close anytime.

. . . I buy canned peas and canned fish in a red sauce—both always reliable—to eat in my hotel room which has both heat and light on this particular visit, for which I am most thankful. Russia's diamond wealth is embedded in Yakutyia. Prisoners of Stalin's gulag mined the ores as well as logged the forests. Many of the townspeople probably are children and grandchildren of the political exiles and common criminals who were sent to mine the ores and log the forests. "Prisoners still do logging here," said the son of the Governor who had the task of chauffeuring me around this morning. Later I asked, "What kind of prisoners are those loggers?" "Prisoners," he shrugged.

I did take Saturdays and Sundays to visit the markets whenever and wherever I happened to be on the surface soils of the gulag. I was especially fascinated by hats: *this hat will cure a headache in ten minutes. . . . That one is squirrel* (the lowliest in value). *. . . This one is lamb. But mink, very fine. But there! The finest! Sable. You want to buy?* This hat for spring; that hat for early winter; another for deep winter, and so forth. I certainly had learned the difference between an ineffective wool hat and a most effective fur hat for keeping away the cold but I couldn't afford a quality fur hat. I could never distinguish on anyone's kept woman who had the sable (that conveyed the highest prestige) and who wore mere mink. Maybe the mink for the party official's wife, maybe sable for his glamorous mistress. *How much do they have to give, these mistresses, to their masters.*

Whenever it was market day for me I dressed *not* to be noticed. I preferred not to be noticed so I could observe things as they were without worrying that anyone would change their behavior because an *Amerikanka* was near. That's not to say I was unattractive; my father was always telling me how beautiful was his daughter, and when I take a look at photos, well . . . there's a certain class, a certain height, a certain slenderness, dark hair, dark eyes, full lips, a quiet yet alluring presence. Yet, over the many years of my travel to Russia, I would take note every now and then—walking here and there on my days off on the streets of whatever town I was in, carrying a plastic tote bag, wearing Russian plastic sandals and a kerchief (if it were summer), or heavy boots and a locally bought affordable *double* angora wool hat (if it were winter), on whatever errand I could conjure up (a needed cosmetic item, a tin of canned fish), on those Saturdays and Sundays when I was no one special—Yes, I would take note that I could well have been Elizaveta, a *Russkaya* from the steppe, instead of Elisa, an *Amerikanka*, from Seattle. I wonder now however, did I really fool anyone? Everyone would sense I was *inorodynye*—not native, not one of us—and most probably they would sense I was a Jew. I didn't think about this then but I feel it now.

Intrepid I was. Yet this was easy work. Offensive to no one. I was doing the Jewish thing but I wasn't announcing myself as Jewish. No markings on me anywhere that might arouse in others that certain residing sense of suspicion or distaste that might interfere with my work: no yarmulke, no necklace with a Jewish star. How peculiar this feels right now. To say it this way. But was I hiding my Jewishness?

I had no sense then of *wanting to feel* my Jewish self/soul doing this work. No desire even to make inquiries: *are there records of who was sent to which camps now that glasnost is in vogue? Would you be willing to talk about this?* No. Nothing like that from me. Those questions were either still inchoate or repressed. I don't know which. Maybe my hosts were waiting for such a question. Maybe they wanted to be asked, not needing to hide anything anymore. Maybe I was the one hiding. Hiding my Jewishness in order to not let that interfere, *because I had a sense it would interfere.* I did not want to jeopardize my work.

But of course the Russians knew. I am sure someone filed a report about my doings on every trip I took. Of course my hosts had their instructions to file a report. I can imagine the conversations:

—*I have filed the report. Details of a meeting between our Hebrew and a certain Professor Burko at the Zalino Hotel on 4 May. Another meeting on 5 May. She received from him two documents.*

—*She is a busybody, isn't she. Our Hebrew. Attracts them like flies. Flies that the Colonel can turn into files. If Olychka won't write anything, then you will continue to do so. Yes. Our American Hebrew is a queer woman. Always so busy-busy. But she's a good promoter. She brings these Americans to us despite our mosquitoes, our plagues.*

—*She's always so cheerful.*

—*Damn if I know why. She's away from her husband? She's in love with Kap-i-tan? She's in love with Lev Alexandrovich? With the mosquitoes? With our plagues? With our Aeroflot? With our trees? With the taiga? God knows.*

I wasn't fooling anyone. Of course I am a Jew, doing Jewish work: instead of peddling dry goods in and around Wilmington, Delaware I am peddling promising business deals in and around a cold faraway place known to most folks as Siberia. I was making friends. A warming in US - USSR relations allowed for this. Business interest was high. I was collecting contacts for future business and match-making, collecting commercial intelligence for the newsletter I and a team of five were now publishing from Seattle for a global readership.

So much to learn! So much to engage in! These field trips of mine had one primary purpose: to connect with folks and to learn as much as I could about needs, proposals, possibilities. To be gracious and in that way to make friends. This was good work, I believed in it. Work which meant accepting the *at least four feet wide* rack of reindeer antlers gifted to me (that gift I left in the airplane's luggage bin) and the wonderful framed collage of walruses grouped in front of an arctic landscape, all done in walrus hide and fur (this I look at on my office wall every day). Work which meant expressing a willingness to participate in the event of the day.

This work came naturally to me. I believed it to be much more than market maker, more than bringing buyer and seller together, more than capitalism's win-win. There was the bigger picture: bringing folks of different cultural habits, different business ethics together to work on a common goal. Building bridges (not the bridges that crossed teeming rivers during spring run-offs, those that our Americans built for the logging trucks to cross year round) but intercultural bridges. I believed then, as I do still, that when peoples "do" together they get to know each other. And the deeper the knowing, the more likely the compassion. *That* mattered.

That trophy-sized rack of antlers was given to me on a day spent near the continental divide in the Arctic circle; the divide identified by the Kolyma River on its west and by the Omolon River on its east. That day's purpose was to celebrate the possibility of building a reindeer meat sausage plant. This plant would be a joint venture between a Russian state farm which managed herds of reindeer and an Alaska business man, Doug Drum. Drum's skills were well known for the fact that his reindeer meat sausage represented the State of Alaska during food fairs at the US White House. To pay him for the investment of know-how and to pay for the American plant and equipment, the Russian side (it was tentatively agreed) would pay with reindeer horn, a very valuable product in Asian markets.

On that bright sunny day, on that high plateau, on that continental divide, everywhere was only white and I knew I was as near to the sky as I would ever be. The day included a special feast of cooked reindeer meat but first, the special toast "to Russian-American cooperation." This toast along with Russian vodka involved a taste of the bone marrow of a freshly killed reindeer. Like in the Peace Corps you do as the natives do. You show a *willingness*. And yes, for me, it all was safe, interesting and sincere work. I wasn't thinking about anything else other than, Can we actually make this project work between our two countries? (No, as it turned out. The answer was No. This project was vetoed just as the paperwork was being finalized. At that moment Moscow's long arm reached across the Eurasian continent to issue an ordinance that prevented any exports of reindeer antlers—to any country at any time.)

My ability to empathize with outsiders and communicate with them served me well in my career. Skilled as an intermediary, this ability became my competitive edge. I became a person who builds bridges, a solid much-approved of role. Not taking sides, my job was to stay neutral between unlike groups. Trying to help unlikes understand each other. Certainly if Russians and Americans, so unlike each other in so many ways, could nonetheless establish business relations with each other, if the two sides could find the win-win and common bonds. Well, that would make for very satisfying work.

13. TAIGA, TUNDRA, GULAG

I couldn't see the Kolyma River Basin from the plateau on the continental divide where our helicopter had parked for our reindeer festivities. And our hosts didn't offer the helicopter for a side trip of views. The Kolyma River flows from the western slopes of the Stanovoi Mountain range then follows a route north to the East Siberian Sea. This marks the continental divide on its west. East from the divide rivers flow down the mountains' eastern slopes into the Anadyr River and then on to the Bering Sea of the Pacific Ocean.

The Kolyma River Basin—the gold mining colonies of the Upper, Middle and Lower Kolyma—served as destination camps for the hard labor punishment of many exiled prisoners. This system has served the Russian (and Soviet, and perhaps post-Soviet) states since the Tsars. In the days of the Tsars, gold was a basis of strength. Yet gold was very far from European Russia, much of it in the Kolyma River Basin in the Arctic Circle, further east than Eastern Siberia. Thus penal labor, or exile to Siberia became a usual punishment for legions of both common and political prisoners.

My maternal grandfather escaped exile to Siberia. My paternal granduncle, Mokha, *evaded* exile. Yes, Mokha evaded the pinchers of the Tsar's secret police; certainly he was in one way or another agitating and/or connected to anti-tsarist, pro-revolutionary activities. We don't know the details. But Mokha was a wheeler-dealer: for the jobs he gets for his relatives and for his travels here and there beyond Gorodische: *shenanigans* his sister Klara declares.

The Russian Tsarist exile system existed for a long century before Stalin ramped it up with his infamous purges of the 1930s. Before the building of the Trans-Siberian Railroad in the early 20th Century, exile usually meant stays in camps in *Western* Siberia; Omsk, for instance, to which the Tsarist government sentenced the writer Fyodor Dostoevsky in 1849, as an enemy of the State.

When the Trans-Siberian Railway reached Irkutsk in *Eastern* Siberia in 1895, prisoners were transported from cities in Western Russia by train to the infamous Aleksandrovsk relay prison near to Irkutsk. From there prisoners trudged by foot or by sleigh to points in Russia's Far

North. How they actually got to these points is more than I can imagine despite descriptions of travel—in the winter over frozen rivers and ice roads, in the summer over swamps and muskeg. Convicts sent north were dispersed at other prisoner relay stations after Aleksandrovsk: Olekminsk in the Territory of Yakutiia, or, Verkhnoyansk, the coldest place on earth. Prisoners sent further to the east and the Far North again relied on foot travel summer or winter. The Kolyma River Basin, that set of camps in the Arctic Circle, was "as far away from the heart of society as the moon."

Let's look at a report of a typical political exile in the days of my grandfather and granduncle.

Prisoner W.

. . . Born in April 1880. Participated in the revolutionary movement since 1896, member of the social democratic movement in Gomel. Was arrested several times, and in 22 April 1901 his case was heard by a special tribunal. After that, by an order of the Ministry of Internal Affairs issued on 7 October 1901, was sentenced to Eastern Siberia for four years.

At first W was to be sent to Irkutsk Oblast, but by order of the Military Governor General of Irkutsk, place of exile was changed to Olekminsk, Yakutiia. W was sent to Olekminsk from the Alexandrovsk relay prison on 30 April 1902.

Arrived at Olekminsk on 4 June 1902. In a short period of time managed to escape three times. First escape was on 27 December 1902. Caught the next day. Second escape was on 13 February 1903. Caught one week later. Then on 29 March 1903, by order of the Yakutsk Governor, sent to Verkhoyansk. However before day of departure, on 22 April 1903, made a third escape. Caught two months later on 20 June in a town eight hundred kms to the west. On 11 of July was sent back to Olekminsk.

By order of the Governor dated 17 July 1903 ordered sent to Kolyma, arrived 27 November 1903. At first was placed in Middle-Kolymsk, and then in Upper-Kolymsk. With the implementation of the Manifesto of August 11, 1904, by order of the Governor General dated 5 November 1904, was released and exile cancelled.

Was sent from Middle-Kolymsk on 25 January. Arrived in Yakutsk 15 March 1905. Received a passport to leave Yakutsk and on 19 March returned to Gomel. Upon return to Gomel continued activities in the ranks of the Russian Socialist Democratic Revolutionary Party, first as a Bolshevik, then as a Menshevik . . . Studied medicine and law . . . An accomplished scientist . . . . . . Died in 1932, killed under a passing train.[1]

As noted in the report, from Aleksandrovsk Relay Station prisoners were sent to Olekminsk, or further north to Verkhoyansk or even farther northeast to the camps of Upper, Middle, and Lower Kolyma . Recently available documents (from which prisoner W's report is taken) show statistics about these exiles during the times of Manya's family. Since Jews were identified as Jews—not Russians, not Poles, not Ukrainians, not anything but Jews—we show up as a category of prisoners sent to these far off places. Jews were the second largest group after Russians to be exiled to Olekminsk in the decade spanning 1895-1905. And third in number (after Russians and Poles) sent to Verkhoyansk. As the Report of Prisoner W shows, despite earlier escapes, Kolmya seemed in that period of time to be . . . a place from which no one escaped.

The area is all *tundra*. Tundra is either mining or reindeer country. Our day-long reindeer festival on the continental divide showed this mostly empty terrain. Inhospitable for most vegetation, certainly not suitable for trees. The image I hold of the tundra—other than very cold with a very short growing season—is a view I did see from our helicopter on our trip back to the small village where we were spending the night. Evensk is a provincial town near the port of Gizhiga on the Sea of Okhotsk. A Russian icebreaker-class cargo ship had plowed a path through the ice to make a delivery of cargo. Every winter the vessel comes to offload a large delivery to the local population. The month was March, well before ice break-up. From the air I could see the vessel surrounded with folks—looking like ants who have just found a stash of bread crumbs—coming and going in trucks, cars, and

90

sleighs offloading the cargo. The surrounding ice was so solid it was all road except for the channel. Imagine an ocean of ice, a coast line, all white, all snow and ice, so that a person can't tell where one stops and the other begins. Imagine a cry lost in all that tangle of ice and snow. Very isolated. Very lonely.

Prisoner W during his two years of exile between 1903 and 1905 lived in the tundra. South of the tundra is *taiga,* also a land of many gulag camps. The completion of the Trans-Siberian railway all the way across Russia to Vladivostok in 1916 allowed the imperial and then the Soviet state to send prisoners by rail to Vladivostok and then—somehow, by boat, by foot—into the gold mining regions of Magadan and from there to the mines of the Kolyma River basin. From Vladivostok north to Magadan—from taiga to tundra—prisoners traveled by boat then by foot. Prisoners at the *taiga* exile camps logged and built roads. Scientists see *taiga* as boreal forest—coniferous forests of larch, spruce, and pine. The Russians see *taiga* as impenetrable forest.

My first sense of the taiga was on a train ride with Vera, my cabin-mate. We had started at Khabarovsk (near the Pacific coast) and were heading westward. I was traveling further than Vera. Her destination was about twenty hours away, her arrival time after midnight. My arrival was more felicitous, early evening the next day. Vera worked as a chief bookkeeper, she told me, saying she had been given three weeks health leave at a sanatorium and that was where she was going.

Russians I knew have a way of accepting the lot they are given at any point in time. It's their way. It's a passive way, but easily understood. It comes, I believe, from a system dominated by power. You either have power (briefly or not) or you don't. It's all a hierarchy of power. I may be a shopkeeper so my power is over the goods that I sell. I do whatever I can with this bit of power, that's all I have. Others have more power, and some a lot. Power at whatever level is arbitrary and can be cruel. Vera was taking a three-week health leave at a sanatorium. What kind of sanatorium it was I would never know. Was it really something she wanted to do? Was she telling me the truth? Her demeanor was polite, even sweet, but concealing. Whatever I knew about my hosts, I believed more was concealed than revealed. Concealed far beyond my reach. Perhaps Vera was someone's favorite

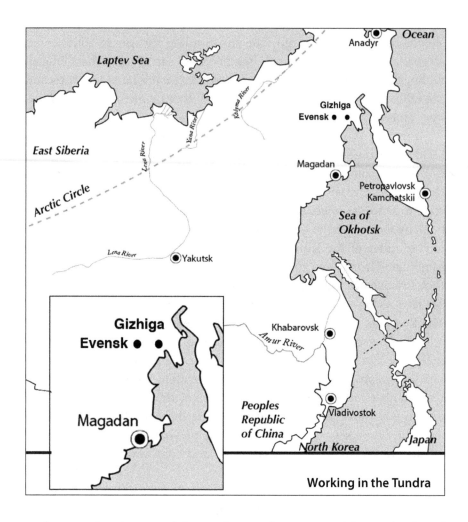

Working in the Tundra

and was going to one of those places where powerful men host and engage their favorite women. When I was invited to spas, mineral hot springs, natural mud bathing resorts, the men I met were with beautiful Russian women, their favorite consorts.

Vera and I shared what food we had brought with us, sipped hot tea offered by the wagon-mistress. When our small window showed only darkness, I took my turn in the washroom, arranged my bedding on my favored upper bunk, climbed up and in, turned on the small light to write a few notes. Not long after, the train stopped for about ten noisy minutes. "They are bringing in coal to keep our wagon warm," Vera said. "Soon it will be very cold outside, at least minus thirty-five."

I knew cold, sort of. I knew it only when I wasn't dressed for it. I knew it at once when the weather had gotten too cold for my double-layered angora wool ski cap lined with the finest angora. The cold went right through it as if I was wearing a silk stocking. I knew it when I stayed out too long one cold night, minus 22 centigrade with not enough protection. The cold started to enter into my core, ignoring what protection I thought I had. For me, overnight train travel — when your cabin mates are kindly, the wagon warm, when your door is lockable, when the wagon-mistress has tea — was always pleasurable. I slept easily, and when I did awake it would be only for a minute during one of the many stops. Some of those stops were quiet — a few low voices, footsteps of a single passenger loading or disembarking. Some were noisy — when a group of passengers embarked or disembarked, or because the local station master yelled from the platform a few words to the wagon-mistress. Some stops were without human voices at all — only the opening and closing of the wagon doors.

That night I woke to see the small light on in Vera's bunk area. I blinked to see Vera — already dressed wrapped up in her fur *shuba*, a wool scarf wound tightly around her neck, fur hat securely in place — standing in the narrow space between the two sets of bunk beds applying lipstick using a tiny mirror. It was 12:30 a.m. She said she'd be getting off at the next stop. I thanked her for the treats she had shared and wished her all the best. She replied in kind, took her suitcase, slid the cabin door open, stepped into the corridor, slid the cabin door closed behind her.

As soon as I had locked the cabin door, the train stopped. I turned to my window, knowing that was the side from which she would exit. I was on the right side of the train to see her but I could see nothing. Just darkness. No station. No station master. No cars. No lights. No persons anywhere. Just the *taiga*, that mighty and silent and empty space. I finally made out a small, well-bundled woman. Vera. The only thing I could make out in that dark night was her standing solitary figure. What happened next. Where she went. Who she met. Where the *taiga* took her, I will never know.

Bundled up warm on a moving train isn't experiencing the *taiga*. Nor is the *taiga* always cold. We were traveling by Land Rover in daylight on an autumn day of warm weather when a flat front tire forced us to stop and fix it. I didn't mind those breakdowns. We had a spare and I had a chance to stretch, walk a few paces away from the car to relieve my bladder, and experience the taiga in ways I never had before. It wasn't the trees, forbs, vines, underbrush, duff, mud, clay, flora, fauna that seemed unusual to me that windless day. No, as I walked far enough away until I no longer heard the men working I knew it was something else. A profound stillness . . . as if I were in the midst of an immensity full of meaning yet silent about that meaning . . . As if I were in a place where we humans weren't needed. A place without human purpose and, particularly, *indifferent* to human purpose. A place with an intense energy I could feel: beneath me from the ground; around me from the brush; above me from the forest canopy. I felt like a visitor in a place that tolerated visitors, that tolerated every other thing foreign to it, but a place that didn't *need* any of it. It was enough as it was on its own. It needed no human to name it, claim it, exploit it, love it, protect it. It accepted our human needs, desires, pains, sufferings, tragedies, longings—without adjustment of any kind. I could feel its vibrations, and if someone had said this is a sacred place, I would have believed it. The *taiga* holds all that has happened with an almost sacred silence. We Jews, too, as a people hold all that has happened to us also with a sense of the sacred. We suffer but we hold.

My indifference at the time to that part of Russian history which had formed the very foundation of life in the region where I was working is astounding. The places, the pieces, the history, the *gulag*, were all *right in front of me*. The City of Vladivostok—once a relay station transferring hundreds of thousands of prisoners from European Russia to worlds "as far away from their society as the moon"—held great *historical* drama, yet I was ignorant and indifferent. Khabarovsk, a city north of Vladivostok, from which most of my travels were made, reached deep into *Gulag* territory.

A good friend I made during my work in Russia tells me of the time he found the remains of a gulag camp on the same ground as was the headquarters of his Russian-American logging joint venture. This logging camp was at Siziman Bay, about an hour's helicopter ride north of Khabarovsk. He and I had many conversations about this.

A FRIEND REMINISCES

Yes, our logging camp was on the same site as where another camp was situated in the days of Stalin. We figured it all out. There were plenty of clues to be found. With a large sockeye salmon run in the Siziman River, this complex was obviously set up to process salted fish. The prisoners cut the timber and logs. Hauled the logs down to the sawmill. The sawmill cut the logs into lumber and barrel staves. The fish were brined in those wood-lined and plastered holes we found in the ground. Barrels of salted fish and perhaps lumber too were trundled out onto a timber pile dock and shipped off to wartime Russia. Except for a few ditches, an indistinct hedge row here and there, and a few wagon ruts, all vestiges of that busy camp have been swallowed up by the taiga. The whole place burned down in 1953, the year Stalin died.

We did find more surprising clues. Our bulldozers uncovered a huge pile of rusted barrel hoop material. We noticed the iron bones of an ancient bulldozer sticking out of the beach at low tide, and a few rotted-off piling stubs above the tide line. The whole Siziman Bay complex came into focus when we found a number of eight-foot diameter wells sunk about 10 feet into the ground behind the hightide level.

. . . . .

Russian topog maps, from 1953, show clusters of little black rectangles back in the boondocks but near our camp. A friend from Idaho and I set out one weekend to explore. Even though thousands of logs were taken out on sleighs or sleigh-trains over the frozen creek beds and meadows, sleighs or by hand, we were still unable to see any trace of human activity. (Later I found the outlines of rotted log sleighs and all the iron fittings and chains exactly where they rotted away on the muskeg parking lot at Siziman Bay.)

My friend and I bushwhacked until I noticed a flattened plane about the creek. . . . Sure enough sticking up through the moss was the single link of a big chain. Then a 10 foot hunk of chain that one man could barely lift. My partner found the campsite. The buildings were completely flattened. Only rotten logs, rusting hinges and bars, and some shallow foundations remained. This and moss-covered piles of logs obviously waiting to be sledded to the mill site. It seems all cutting and skidding of logs to this camp was done by hand. A more brutal kind of back-breaking work, I cannot conceive.

Immediately above this camp stood the most beautiful 40-year old pure spruce timber stand I had ever seen in the area. Why? My guess is this was the site where all the heavy moss was stripped off of the ground to chink the cabin walls, insulate the ceilings and probably insulate the beds and clothes of the prisoners to keep them alive through the winter. The lightweight spruce seeds will germinate very nicely when the moss and duff are removed from the forest floor.[2]

▲ Site of former gulag camp at Siziman Bay

Notes

1   P. L. Kazaryan, *Olekminskaia Politicheskaia Ssylka*: *1826–1917* [Olekminsk region as place of political exile: 1826–1917] (Yakutsk, Russia: Rossiiskaia Akademiia Nauk, 1995), 302–303.
2   N. Brocard, "Exploring Former Gulag Sites in Khabarovskii Krai," *Russian Far East Update* (August 1998): 10.

14. Papa, Come Home!

$\mathcal{T}$rying to understand the period between 1918 and 1921 in Manya's life is like trying to understand the depths of my situation at home—so many different battles being fought, so many layers of complexities.

In the case of the Russian Civil War between 1918 and 1921, in the arena where Gorodische is located, five major events take prominence.

First Major Set of Events
The collapse of the Tsarist State and its Imperial Armed Forces. This political and military collapse let loose dragoons of soldiers and officers to roam throughout Russia's Ukrainian Southwestern Provinces. Suddenly out of work, some of these men simply put down their arms and went home. Others *kept* their arms and went home. Yet another group kept their arms *and* their military posture to look for new deployment under another flag or banner. The region and its capitol city Kiev was suddenly under-defended and soldiers and officers were ready for hire.

Second Major Set of Events
The resurgence of the Ukrainian National Independence Movement. This movement, under multiple uniforms and at various times under different and competing leaders, was waiting to reassert itself. Long in existence, long in passion, long simmering, long revengeful, long anti-Semitic, almost immediately upon the collapse of the Tsar, forces rose from subterranean cover to forge a fight for an independent Ukraine with Kiev as its capitol.

Third Major Set of Events
The end of World War I. The meetings at Brest-Litovsk where the German and Austro-Hungarian powers agreed to a ceasefire in Russia's Ukrainian Provinces in exchange for Lenin allowing them continuing occupation encompassed all of 1918. The Germans wanted desperately to maintain a supply of food coming from the fertile Ukrainian soil to feed its ever weakening armies. But the Treaty of Versailles in June

1919, pronouncing the total defeat of Germany and Austro-Hungary, overwhelmed all the earlier events. The Axis defeat left hundreds of thousands of German, Austrian, and Hungarian soldiers stranded. The efforts to return home from locations far flung on both sides of the Dnieper River were met with armed hostilities. The lack of a functioning transportation system made the situation worse for the already weakened state of the occupying troops. Local militias found a good source of weapons winning skirmishes and even battles with these defeated and retreating troops.

Fourth Major Set of Events

Rise of the Bolsheviks. The Bolsheviks, vanguard of both the ideological and the military wings of Russia's Socialist Revolutions, now lead the local (even if uncontrollable) partisan armies, and all the regiments of Trotsky's Red Army. The goal of party leaders was to cede to no one control of the Ukraine and most importantly not to lose Kiev. This set of events set the stage for Bolshevik battles not only against those who want Ukraine independent but battles against strong anti-Bolshevik forces, also called Whites (or the Monarchists or Imperialists). And later an aggressive neighbor, Poland.

Fifth Major Set of Events

An awakened, armed, autonomous, and unpredictable peasantry. Awakened by the vacuum of power and the propaganda of the day, the peasant—whether he be anti-landlord, anti-authority, anti-urban, anti-Semite, anti-requisitioning, or anti-Bolshevik—was always being wooed by any of the many local military leaders (Cossacks, anarchists, guerillas, bandits, or "crazies") crisscrossing the region, making for forces most destructive and most unpredictable.

Let's imagine now a set of slides as if I were preparing a slide show. If these five sets of events were each able to be captured separately on its own transparency and then the five were placed one on top of the other, anyone trying to look through all five at once would see only chaos. Nothing would be understood. The only way to even begin would be to slide out each transparency one at a time and look, all the while knowing that *no single transparency without the others can explain the situation alone.*

The final picture *under* these five slides or transparencies if we *were* able to make it out would be a boiling cauldron of various and opposing armies or groups of armed men attended by

overt mutinies,

desertions to home,

refusals to carry out orders,

unsanctioned establishment of local organs of power,

defections, and

changing alliances.

More to the point, the skirmishes, battles, raids, uprisings, points of contact were usually narrowed to the filigree of rail lines running between the villages and cities—from one direction or another— toward Kiev. *This fact is essential to our understanding of Manya's family. Gorodische was a station on the rail line which, as it approached Kiev, brought transport from the south (the Black Sea ports), from east of the Dnieper (from heartland Russian cities of Kharkov and Rostov-on-Don) as well as from points west.*

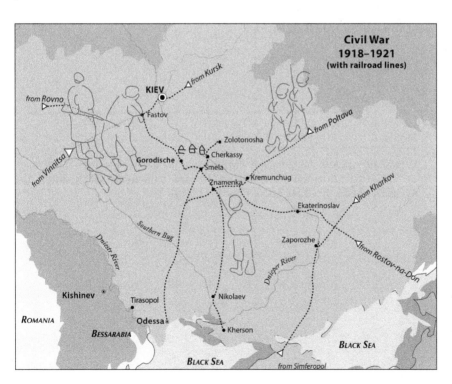

So how to describe the impact on Manya's family? Maybe best to just say theft, murder, rape, total destruction. But that can't get at the feeling of the waves of threat coming toward them time after time during these years. No matter who the soldiers were, all were wary, hungry, sodden, ill-fed, ill-equipped, ill-clothed, even feral.

The Ukraine at this time was "less a bounded territorial entity than a loose confederation of pulsating peasant autonomies and wandering regiments" writes M. Akulov in his Harvard doctoral dissertation.[1] Maybe it was better that Eli didn't know the details despite the suffering he had to have felt being distant and out of touch.

Manya's second oldest son, Meer, joined the Red Army sometime after 1917. And thereafter was lost. There was never information about how or where he died except that (from what my father told me) his canteen was returned to the family. The canteen that my father had always kept on his desk to hold pencils, always nicely sharpened. Toward the end of his life in a new apartment, my father had moved the canteen to a place on his kitchen counter. After he died an agency came to clear out the kitchen and I guess the few things of value there went unnoticed into a dumpster.

Notes

[1]   Mikail Akulov, *War without Fronts: Atamans and Commissars in Ukraine, 1917–1919* (doctoral dissertation, Harvard University, 2013), http://nrs.harvard.edu/urn-3:HUL.INstRepos:11181181.

15. JEWISH PASSION, JEWISH SUFFERING

*K*lara writes (after the letters resume in 1921) that the family is trying to find out about Meer who is now a soldier, but lost. Of course, I think, he would be lost. A circumcised man amongst Russians (who do not practice circumcision) is no different than sewing a yellow star on an outer garment. You are announcing your difference. And despite any and all pronouncements that Trotsky's Red Army would not tolerate anti-Semitism (after all, Trotsky was born Jewish), the Ukrainian peasant—when drunk and uninhibited—cannot so obey. Alcohol and the Ukrainian peasant-soldier created frenzy and we Jews were the victims. My father's brother, Meer Brodiansky, changed his name to Michael Bonderenko (a native Ukrainian name) on the chance this would help. It didn't. No one knows the circumstances of his death because he was never heard from again after he enlisted. This boy of 19 was naive to hope that his revolutionary zeal might deter the base instincts of the Russian peasant.

There is no place to run. We choose to identify ourselves.

"Take the covenant, Elisa," says the rabbi who gave my children their Jewish education. He had agreed to have a one-hour phone conversation even though he doesn't fulfill rabbinical duties any more due to age and illness. "Your soul, Elisa, is asking you to take the covenant and go further in your Jewish understanding. What's the risk? " he asks. "It's just a next step. You are going to just try and see. Give it a trial. You have to try. All this takes place in time, and you can't circle too long. You have much to give to others. We are a civilization of 3800 years. Be a part of your people. Keep it going. If you do nothing and stay where you are, you will have crossed no bridges.

"You say you love Judaism. But it is only our actions that make us who we are. And actions are uncertain enterprises. Take the risk, and you will then come to understand. My reading of the Hebrew in the passage *Exodus 24:7*," he continued, "is God asked us to do and then to understand or hear." This beloved rabbi was very kind to give me his time. His words stay with me.

Yet, even though I had insisted on the bar/bat mitzvah of my son Amos and daughter Rachael; even though I was so proud of the sentence during that event when I, their mother, pass the Jewish tradition on to them; even though almost all of the Passover seders in my adult life were held from my kitchen; even so it seems I was much more comfortable inviting non-Jews for Passover than in actually mixing with Jews. I wanted these guests to know we are not Christians but in a setting that was comfortable and peaceful. I wanted to announce my Jewishness but without having to *join* anything. So, even though I loved making custom-designed Haggadah covers for our Passovers; even though I only missed one Passover in my whole life, including during travel; even though it was I who designed the collage which is the centerpiece for the *ketubah* of my daughter's marriage to her husband that now hangs beautifully over their bed; even so I shrink— yes shrink—from active participation in a synagogue. I could not say, and still cannot say: Yes I want to belong to a Jewish community.

I am trying. Maybe, I say to myself, I do not have to stay separate even though this separateness has run through the entire course of my life, has become a way of life. It worked, you must understand, because I was nonetheless connecting. I was using my non-connectedness to connect one group to another. Not a part of any group but a go-between, a bridge, instead. So I was making connections. Connections of a particular sort. There is connecting in the sense of the work I did, but now I see there is another sense of connecting to something in me buried very deep. When I try the temple, most of the time now I do not spill tears, for I am busy trying to decipher a Hebrew word or two. Words I have recently learned. Nonetheless when the Torah is brought out and carried around the room (*hakafah*) for the congregants to touch and kiss it and there is much joy from the congregation, I cry. Am I crying because I am home?

I am conflicted because my parents' marriage held so much disagreement between them. I can easily imagine my mother's firm rejection of religious Judaism. She never talked about Judaism as a religion or even delineated any moral teaching that was traced to our religion. (The only thing she did mention was anti-Semitism and only once: when I, a naïve and innocent fifteen-year old, was not admitted to a teen-club formed under the umbrella organization, the Daughters of the American Revolution. And with respect to that I think she was right to explain to me my rejection, for I felt it deeply.) I can and do *remember* my mother's defiance, but I can *feel* my father's solace when he is reading a Hebrew book of prayers with his prayer shawl on. I never remember approaching him at these moments but I would notice. I can't say I fingered his *tallit* which is somewhat surprising because I have always been tactile. I know he took comfort reciting Hebrew prayers. I have a desire to unite with him in his religiosity, yet again and again I will not betray my mother or her values.

My Circumcised Grandson—a note

"I've heard that circumcision is mutilation" were the words I was sure she had pronounced, this exceptional mother of my son's newborn boy. This wonderful woman who I so admired for her attentive joyful way of mothering (including a home birth with garlands and candles). She was not born Jewish and knew absolutely nothing about us as a faith, nation, culture, civilization. She *did* know her son was to be celebrated, but expressed real fear of circumcision.

Maybe she and my son had planned to have this discussion during the walk we were taking because both grandmothers were present. Maybe my son needed some back-up. Clearly his partner was hesitant and fearful about circumcision. I however had only one position, not negotiable. Of course, Aditieh had to be circumcised. *That's what we do. That's what Jews do.* Above all else, this is what we do. I didn't waffle. I didn't think twice. It is just what we do, I relayed. My counterpart, Aditieh's other grandmother, not Jewish, presented the issue with a neutrality. Her husband was circumcised but not her son. Or the reverse, her husband was not, but her son was. (I don't remember which.) Nonetheless she presented the issue as a choice. For me, there was no choice.

16. A Terrible Night

*E*very Jewish soul living in the Russian Pale would be aware of the threat of *pogroms*—those sudden outbursts of violence against Jewish villagers involving drunken peasants, complicit local authorities, and armed marauders. Manya's oldest daughter Rivka alludes to this in a postcard in 1917 where she writes to her father: "*Shavuot* has passed without any incidents." *Pogroms* are not new to the civil war years we are focusing on. What was new were the *uninhabited* seats of power that limited any checks to the *uninhibited* anti-Semitism once again in open currency.

The years of civil war in the Ukraine, especially 1919 and 1920, were years of extreme violence by various armed groups upon Jewish village populations. Gorodische was no exception. As I have explained, the vacuum of power brought by the tsarist collapse provided many empty avenues for the rise of various and competing groups seeking political control, seeking tangible property, seeking self-government, havoc, anarchism, vengeance. Armies, regiments, Cossack-led/peasant-filled militias, groups of bandits and "crazies" all swarmed about.

The largest groups were three: those fighting for Ukrainian National Independence, those fighting for the establishment of Soviet (Bolshevik) power, and those seeking the restoration of Imperial Power. Each of these three groups had clear policy objectives. But the region was aswarm also with petty, powerful and well-armed demagogues. Men who had the trust of a local peasant village or a conglomerate of local peasant villages. Men who sought power for power's sake, influence for influence's sake. Men whose policy positions were anarchistic, autonomous, amorphous, and always changeable.

The peasant generally defined his self-interest apolitically. Centuries of oppression taught him that. But in these years his passions were aroused by the slogans of agitators: Down with the landlord! Power to the countryside! No rights to the German invaders! No rights to the new Soviet socialist requisitioners! *Who is the enemy? Jews!*

The demagogues took advantage of the peasant's passions. Fierce fighters of the Cossack brand, they opted for self-aggrandizement. They took for themselves and for their soldiers the bounty (supplies and weapons) from their military victories. They armed their peasant soldiers. They fought for the glory of victory and for influence. Their allegiances were fickle—giving, then taking back, support—whether it be for Ukrainian National Independence, for Soviet power, or for the restoration of Imperial power. These leaders improvised. They were stridently autonomous, changing alliances at random. Add to those demagogues the bandits and crazies and, finally, the exhausted and starving soldier, we know the Jewish populations of the village were not safe from anyone.

Not safe from the Imperialists, always anti-Semitic.
Not safe from the aroused peasant.
Not safe from the Nationalist Ukrainian or Cossack.
Not safe from the exhausted soldier at the end of his rope.

These leaders of the peasant militia were men who wanted to hold the power of position, or the power of place, or the power of influence. But to get the peasant willing to fight, these leaders needed reasons. *Get the property of the landlords!*—one reason. *Get the property of the rich townspeople!*—another. Fight against the Germans who want to take their crops, or the agents of the Soviet socialist revolution who want the same.

Kill the Jew! Who for generations had managed the great Polish estates spread throughout the Ukrainian-speaking lands; who had represented the Polish landlords until Catherine the Great, partitioning Poland, kicked the landholding gentry out.

Kill the Jew! Who was twinned with the socialist revolutionary ideology when that ideology went against the peasant during the early years of Leninist policies. Soviet agents requisitioned food throughout the Ukrainian countryside. Many of these agents were Jews.

These Cossack leaders of the village peasant were beneficiaries of the vacuum of power and grew in robustness due to their ability to self-rule and self-supply their troops (primarily from weapons confiscated or laid down by the retreating German occupiers). Their use of anti-Semitic slogans became louder in direct proportion to what they saw as the intrusion of the Leningrad-based, Jewish-based, Soviet power in *their* Ukrainian affairs.

One of the men, Nikifor Grigoriev, was responsible for two pogroms in Manya's village of Gorodische in May 1919.[1] Grigoriev at first saw his role to support the leaders of the Ukrainian National Independence movement. But as the Civil War progressed and Bolshevik propaganda spread, Grigoriev saw the peasantry was less interested in Ukrainian national sovereignty and more interested in joining the class struggle against the propertied class. And so he switched his alliance to the Bolsheviks in 1919. The Bolsheviks, trying to build a fighting force sufficient to meet its enemies (Ukrainian Nationalists and anti-Soviet forces who wanted to restore the former status-quo), took what help they could get from these militiamen who were good fighters and essentially better fortified due to their ability to self-supply their needs.

The Bolsheviks, to combat the growing threat of the counter-revolutionary forces under the command of General Anton Denikin, needed the support of the peasant armies even though they knew these local militia leaders such as Grigoriev could not be much trusted. The Bolsheviks knew the characteristics of these men: too autonomous, with too much of a "treasonable tendency toward recalcitrance."[2] The relationship was tense. Finally, the Soviet Communist Party leaders in Leningrad saw these insurgent-partners like Grigoriev as not able to be reformed into the disciplined players they needed. The Communist Red Army strategists needed to cut ties. Grigoriev knew that. On May 1, 1919 Grigoriev rebelled and attacked an armored train, the *"Kiev-Communist,"* stopped at a station not far from Gorodische, using anti-Semitic slogans—*Down with the Bolsheviks! Down with the Jews!* In the same frenzied state of rebellion, Grigoriev's men enter Gorodische on May 11, 1919. With no higher authority in place except what was at the village level, and with the village authorities complicit in their support of the pogrom—we Jews were helpless.

These *pogromschiks* killed the step-grandmother of Manya's children; wounded her brother (Veniamin the dentist) who lost his arm; and left her children dumb struck as they watched these men sadistically cut out the tongue of their cousin Shimeon after pulling him out from his hiding place under a bed.

106

MY FIRST POGROM

I wake up choking. The window is open but instead of the sweet morning air, I get smoke in my throat. My mother is weeping. I hear her say: "A terrible night, a terrible night. If only your father were here." I dress hurriedly. By the time I sit down to my kasha and warm milk, mother is gone. Where, I ask. To the hospital, says Ida. Then mother will go to grandfather's house. Then to see our cousin Shimeon.

My sister Ida takes me firmly by the hand and we're off to the market place. Everything in the streets smells of smoke, even the trees. "There were fires all night," Ida says. As we get closer to the market place, we push through tall walls of people. They weep, shout and run. The stores and shops smoulder. The smoke hurts my eyes and we go to a side street, toward the synagogue. But there is no synagogue—only pieces of wall. Prayer books are scattered for a block. Old men with beards collect them, gently, by hand, and pile them into small heaps. Each one gives off thin streaks of smoke.

I get close to one of the piles of prayer books. I take a long stick and begin poking. The top pages are half-burned off and the edges of the books are charred. When I push the stick into the pages and turn them over, I can see the Hebrew letters. "It's hard to burn a book," someone says. One of the old men sees me poking into the books, becomes alarmed, rushes over to me and says: "You mustn't. The books are holy." We move on. Ida tells me that after all the prayer books are collected, the men will conduct a funeral for them.

"A funeral?" I ask.

"Yes, just like for a person. Just like they're going to have for Grandmother."

"Is Grandmother dead?"

"She was killed last night. She was shot in the neck. But she had time to get a pillow, and her prayer book, and lie down on the floor in the room where you sleep when you are at Grandfather's. Then she died. Mom said so."

"Is that why Mother went to the hospital?"

"No. She went to see Uncle Veniamin. He's there, wounded. He was looking out the door to see what was going on and they shot him in the arm. They are going to cut it off today. And do you know what happened to cousin Shimeon? They cut out his tongue."

"Will he be able to eat?" I ask. Ida didn't know, but she was sure he wasn't going to be able to talk.

All through the day I heard the word "pogrom." That is what it was. Bands of peasants had come to the Jewish part of the town during the night and, with thunderous shouts and scattering firebrands, began devastating the houses, garden, stores, and anything that belonged to Jews. It was a wild night of killing, shooting and arson. For some reason, the bands did not turn down toward our little street. I had slept through this first pogrom.

Yet . . . yet . . . It was not that pogrom but one in 1920 that devastated Manya's family. General Anton Denikin, Commander of the pro-Tsarist counter-revolutionary forces, and a base anti-Semite, was the instigator this time, according to family notes. Mokha writes (after letters resume) that it was this pogrom during the fall of 1920 that caused the family to flee. The military theatre around Kiev was the scene of a new development during the civil war year of 1920: Polish involvement. Forces seeking a national independent Ukraine joined with a newly established post-war Polish government to try to dislodge the hold the Bolsheviks had on Kiev that year and thus seize control. The Poles remembered the times of pre-partition Poland, before Catherine the Great kicked them out, when the rich Ukrainian farmlands were theirs. The Nationalist Ukrainians were willing to take their chances aligning with the Poles. In May, 1920, the Polish army was able to reach Kiev, but the victory was short-lived. The Poles soon retreated.

According to family notes I have, it was General Denikin, a fierce anti-Semite, who led a pogrom that destroyed the Jewish community of Gorodische. But I cannot be sure. Troop movements were many and complex. Soviet armies advancing, retreating. Polish armies advancing, retreating. By the fall of 1920, the Soviet Red Army was winning battles south of Kiev against the White (pro-Imperialist) armies now commanded by General Wrangel (who had replaced Denikin). Makhno, a powerful Cossack leader who had replaced Grigoriev, was now aiding the Bolsheviks in their fight against General Wrangel's counter-revolutionary forces. Maybe Wrangel's men "stopped" in Gorodische. Maybe the Soviets themselves stopped in Gorodische. Maybe it was Makhno's men. The Cossack Makhno had been fighting on the side of the Red Army but that relationship turned sour and the Red Army was now declaring this man their enemy. Makhno, peeved, irritable and volatile might well have provoked his men to take "revenge"—of any kind.

It could have been the Red Army Cavalry, it could have been an errant peasant militia, it could have been another regiment of the Soviet Armed Forces (even with Jewish soldiers), it could have been retreating Poles, it could have been a group of pro-Tsarist Whites now under General Wrangel. But we know that Manya's flight was sudden and ill-prepared. Mokha writes from the city of Gomel, "We are spread everywhere, and we cannot help each other." Veniamin writes from the city of Kiev, "We are hungry, cold, barefoot."

I know the family left Gorodische just as the *pogromschiks* were burning all the Jewish houses in Gorodische. I know because my father told that story in an essay he wrote about how their escape was interrupted because his mother needed to go back to the fiery scene in order to retrieve her *ketubah*. Her *ketubah* which I now have.

Am I the appointed caretaker of our family history?

So the meaning of a memory finally becomes clear. My father and I are standing on the second floor balcony of our house on 1833 Lamont Street in Washington, DC watching a house burn about two blocks away. My father is holding my hand. Tightly, intensely. We are both silent. I sense something deep, very deep in the way my father was holding my hand. Now I know he was reliving the day his family fled from their burning home. He was ten years old. I am also ten years old.

I was never told. I never heard the word anti-Semitism. I never heard the word *Holocaust* not until I was 21 years old and it came randomly from an old Jewish Russian-language professor of mine. I was blithely ignorant.

But of course — who would want to give these messages to one's children? Who would want to stuff *that* into our souls.

How do I hold it now?

Notes

1   Elias Heifetz, *The Slaughter of the Jews in the Ukraine in 1919* (New York: Thomas Seltzer, 1921), 68, 111, Cornell University Library Digital Collections.
2   Akulov, *War without Fronts.*

MY SECOND POGROM

I remember eating a slice of bread with jam spread on it very lightly, which my mother told me was my lunch. I must have fallen asleep after that, because I recall that suddenly all around me voices were coming from the dark.

"Is it night?" I asked.

"No, darling," my mother answered. "It is day."

"Then where is the sun?"

Mother began to weep. "There are murderers out there. Hooligans. Pogromschiks. We're in danger. Oh, if only your father were here."

I looked about the house. Each window, I could see dimly, was covered with a cloth, black or gray. Oscar [Isor], my oldest brother, was standing at the door, his ear pressed hard against it. "Quiet. No talking," Oscar said. "I hear voices but they're far away."

They'll come," my mother wailed. "They'll kill us. They'll burn the house. If only your father . . . Oh, Eli, why have you left us. Great God, help. If your father were here."

Oscar turned angrily on mother. "Stop it. You'll give us away. And what could father do? We'd still be in trouble." As long as Oscar was with us, I wasn't afraid. He gave orders. He told us what to do.

"Ida, get dressed. Remember what I told you. We'll get you out into the street from the rear window. Go toward the market place. Don't talk to anyone, but if you must, talk Ukrainian, not Russian. But run from anyone who asks you questions."

In a minute or two Ida was dressed in a peasant skirt and blouse—old and tattered. When she put a flowering kerchief about her face, covering her nose almost completely I couldn't recognize her.

Mother pulled Oscar away from the door. "What are you doing? You're sending my child out to be killed. I won't let you. She'll stay."

Oscar became red with anger. He pushed mother aside in fury and pushed Ida toward the window in back of the house. He spoke to her very quietly, but firmly.

"You look like a peasant girl. They won't bother you. Look about you and listen. Find out what's going on. If they're selling anything in the market, buy bread, buy cheese. Talk as little as possible. Your name, if anyone asks, is Tanya. Remember, now, it's not Ida. Tanya. Here's money."

He opened the rear window and Ida disappeared into the street. Mother collapsed into a bed. We waited in fear. Mother looked pale and exhausted. Becky [Rivka] covered her with a thin blanket. Joe [Iosif] sat quietly in a corner. I followed Oscar about the room, holding on to his hand whenever I could.

He was pacing from window to window, listening for sounds from the street. Again, he placed his ear against the door. Then he lifted the table and propped it against the door. He sent us all into the rear room, told us to keep quiet, while he remained at the door, a sentinel.

Suddenly he jumped to the window through which Ida had gone out into the street. "She's back," he said. Ida climbed into the room, out of breath. "They're coming this way. Soldiers. Five or six. They didn't see me. But I saw them point to our street. A peasant was telling them something, pointing to our house. I ran through backyards. They look mean."

Oscar became agitated. He ordered Mother to stay in bed. He told Becky to bring out any medicine bottles we had. He told Ida to take off her peasant dress and hide it. "If they break in, we must tell them we have a sick mother, no father, no money."

There was a vicious banging on the door. My heart stopped. I looked at Oscar. He seemed paralyzed. "Open—or we'll burn this place to the ground," came a voice from the street. Suddenly, soldiers filled our little house. They ripped the blankets off the windows and smashed the panes. They ignored mother and her groaning. They poked into corners, behind curtains, under the beds. "Where's the money? Where are your furs? Your good samovar—not that piece of junk—where is it?" Groans, cries, and whimpers were our reply.

"There's nothing here. Let's go," said a soldier.

"Oh, yes, there is." I looked up to see who was speaking. Later I was told he was a lieutenant. He was neatly dressed. He was in command. "Yes, there's something very good here." He looked at Oscar with a strange smile. "You, my dear, Mr. Young Jew, you're coming with me."

Mother lurched up in her bed with a terrifying shriek. "No, no, you mustn't say this, you mustn't do this. I have no husband. The children have no father. He's our breadwinner. He's so young."

"My dear Mrs. Jewess," said the lieutenant, "it's because he's young that I want him. He'll come with me. He'll be all right. I'll take care of him."

"Children, children," wailed my mother, "weep, beg, implore this good man not to take your brother."

Each of us lunged toward Oscar, grabbing at his arms, legs, waist. Weeping and shrieking, we drew him toward the back of the room, away from the soldiers. The lieutenant seemed amazed at the tumult we made. He stood perplexed, took off his military cap, scratched his head, and shrugged his shoulders. "The devil take it all," he said. Suddenly, our house was empty, the soldiers gone. Only mother's whimpering was heard through the rooms.

* * * * *

We stayed shut in our house for several days. We keep as quiet as we could, slept during the day and night and ate whatever Ida could bring us. In the morning Ida would put on her tattered peasant clothes, climb through the rear window, disappear, later to return with three eggs, a small herring , or a pound of buckwheat groats for kasha.

One day Ida came back frightened. "Someone saw me. He followed me," she said.

Oscar rushed to the doors, now barricaded with the table and chairs, as it had been for days. He listened, but heard nothing. I began to play cat's cradle with Joe.

* * * * *

Just when it finally happened, whether it was Sabbath or a weekday, morning or afternoon, I don't know. I'd been asleep—sleeping was about the only thing to do. Mother woke me, gave me a small slice of bread, and said, "We're leaving. They're burning down the Jewish houses one by one."

Oscar was in command again. He was whispering, but every word of his made me want to cry. "Get ready, quickly," he said. "When you're outside, run down the hill and toward the side road. Faster. I hear voices coming this way."

Becky and Ida scrambled through the window and were gone. Joe jumped after them. Mother lifted me up and out and pushed me forward. Suddenly, she rushed back into the bedroom. I waited outside, in brilliant sunshine.

I could hear Oscar's angry voice inside: "Mom, go, go, move, outside. They're coming."

I looked about, but mother was still inside the house. I could hear her. "I must find it. I must take it," she kept saying. I decided to run after Becky, Ida and Joe. Then, turning around, I saw mother. She held a white handkerchief in her hand. I stopped to wait for her. Then I heard crash of glass and a pounding. The sounds came from our house. I saw Oscar scramble out through the window. He rushed toward me and mother, urging us on. "Run, run, they're here."

Becky and Ida were already far ahead. Joe kept up with them. Oscar urged me and mother on. We kept running down a hill and soon I couldn't see our house at all. Then something happened. I fell. I tried to get up and couldn't. My legs wouldn't hold me up. Mother rushed to me and picked me up. I didn't want to be carried. I was a big boy, ten years old. But Oscar kept ordering, "Move, run! Soon we'll be too far for them to see us." He ran ahead to see that Becky, Ida and Joe were on the right road. Mother groaned. I was a heavy load for her. She had lifted me, with a deep sigh, and I could feel her body laboring under my weight. I saw other people, our neighbors, running behind us, stretched out in a long, thin line. I felt safer. Here, behind us, were our neighbors—they would protect us from the hooligans. Then I saw a fearful sight. Our house was on fire. The houses around ours were also aflame. That was my last sight of Gorodische.

* * * * *

17. It Is My Turn Now to Try

*A*fter I got my PhD I applied for a special exchange program which, if awarded, would mean I would be the first-ever American researcher officially allowed and supported for work in the Russian Far East. My academic women friends gave me a dinner party to congratulate me on my award. I am sure every one of them was doing research of the caliber that would only benefit from a reprieve from teaching and an opportunity to focus. That my research was in the Russian Far East (Siberia, to them) made it more exotic than the laboratories that these science-minded friends were working in. And yes, the candles on the table, their support . . . it felt celebratory.

But at home it was different. My husband balked. He would be saddled with the care of our twelve-year old son. (My daughter now 17 was already staying with friends.) He did not try to forbid me but in every way registered objection. He balked. I balked. *I cannot now retreat. I cannot now yield to the usual impossibility of these things. I cannot now give up this award after all the work and effort of the application process and the trust folks have put in my abilities. I cannot now yield and say I am so sorry but I have to stay home after all. No, it is my turn now. For my grandmother? For my mother? For my daughter? I cannot retreat now.*

The month or so before I was scheduled to depart for my research exchange stay, my husband and I discussed whether our 12-year old son should come with me. The question was: Which would work better for him? To be with me, or to stay with his father? I was thrilled Amos might come with me and thus experience four months of a wholly new culture, broaden his vision, etc. I don't remember my son's involvement in this discussion. Did we even ask him? I inquired of the granting agency: Could he come with me? They inquired of the US governmental commission which in turn inquired of its Soviet counterpart. Even when the answer came—"We are sorry but we cannot bear the cost of your son"—even as I knew my husband was against my going, I knew I could not not go. My personal defense narrative became more fixed. *Other husbands would be able to handle this. There is only integrity, innocence, inspiration in my work, nothing not to be trusted in my leaving.*

What does my husband have to fear? Of course I will return. Surely a solid supportive husband could handle affairs while I was gone. Surely he should be proud to have such a wife.

I simply would not see his point of view. That it *was* otherwise. That my husband was not feeling able to cope. *Surely the family can stay intact for the first month, then they will come to visit me. It is planned, tickets for their trip are ready to be paid for. Okay, just my son and his father.* My daughter chose not to come. She was seventeen and had many interests beyond her parents' dilemmas.

This had started years before, this marital confusion, but had remained subterranean. I, not wanting to see, had put on blinders. Not wanting to feel, I wrapped myself in delusions. *I will take my research trip to the University of Illinois while my son is at YMCA camp. I will not be able to pick my son up from his YMCA week long camp, but his father will pick him up and then I will see him and then we will go on our family vacation.*

Yet I *knew. I knew* while I was at away for those two weeks in Urbana, Illinois, I knew something was not right. I had left them. And they were not coping well. One day after the first week away I let the utter devastation of that felt reality enter into my body and into the room where I was lodged. I stayed inside all afternoon skipping dinner, stunned by a reality—a feeling—I had not wanted to face. When I finally left my small room to seek something to eat, evening had come. Along with a delicate summer sunset, the sky had filled with magnificent large multi-colored air balloons of such color and grandeur. My spirits shouted relief. I took it for a good sign. I reinstated my defense, my blinders: *I will not be able to pick my son up from his YMCA week long camp, but his father will pick him up and then I will see him and then we will go on our family vacation to Grandma and Grandpa's house.*

But our family vacation didn't go as I had imagined. The storms between my husband and myself—whatever the reasons that initiated them—had reached into my son's soul, had knocked him around pretty hard. We were in the living room of my father's house in Old Saybrook, Connecticut. A room made serenely peaceful by Mary, his wife now for almost twenty years. They had just hosted a picnic for the Connecticut Poetry Society which publishes the *Connecticut River Review, A National Journal of Poetry.*

The large screened-in porch adjacent to the living room with its doors opened wide helped the garden scents waft in on the lovely summer afternoon. That porch also housed Mary's collection of poinsettias, now dormant but kept green and alive since the Christmas season past. Amos was on the couch.

"Mom, my stomach hurts really bad."

"How does it hurt my dear sweet boy?"

"Like it has a hole in it. . . . *Really bad*, Mom."

"We'll go to the doctor, Azy-o. I am so sad for you that it hurts like there is a hole in it. But I am here now, my son. I am here now for you."

I try now, years later, to parse my anger. What precisely did that anger mask? Was it a drive to live a life that now was being thwarted by a husband whose lifelessness was on full display? How unbearable for me to see that. My sadness for him was as deep as a Jewish soul can go; for life is to be purposeful, is to be useful, is to repair a world that is in need. It's a felt obligation. My husband's childhood was full of abuse. His soul left helpless by that abuse. I was not able to feel the depression that encompassed him, I was afraid. I would not enter into his blackness. I didn't understand. I didn't want to understand.

My soul needed a new kitchen window, not so the neighbors would see a new kitchen window but because sunlight is important. Yes, it is *very* important.

My soul needed the other half of the steps leading to the basement to be painted. (The job my husband started.) Because it matters that jobs get finished. My soul needs to write, to record; to make images with color because colors—like a vase of freshly cut flowers—bring joy.

What is foreign to my soul and what is basic to it?

I need to rest in the shade of my soul. I do not need to rest in the arms of someone watching television.

I am crazy?

I am madness?

No I am soul speaking.

Soul seeking comfort.

Are there no answers?

There are no answers.

How much is gained when souls thrive.

How much is lost when souls shrivel.

18. The Soul Suffers

*D*uring the military, political and economic mayhem that was revolution, civil war, and the closing chapter of World War I, my father received a letter from his father. This is the only letter from Eli extant that dates from the three civil war years 1918, 1919, and 1920. My father, Benyamin (no longer called Niuma), kept this letter, packing it with the belongings he took with him to America, keeping it his whole life.

Before I even try to imagine Eli's situation, his mind-state, his heart-state as he writes this letter to his son who has just turned eight years old, I am struck by the way he dates this letter: 1918 October 9, Wednesday — The portion of the Torah (*Noah*). I ask my friend Michal to help me understand. Here again is new Jewish learning for me. The kind of Jewish learning I like. So I learn that pious Jews add the title of the portion of the Torah being read during the calendar week of the letter's date. The Hebrew word for Torah portion is *sidra*. Or *sedra*. Also transliterated as *sidrah*, or *sedrah*.

Eli must have been at Synagogue reading with his fellow Jews the weekly *sedrah* for October 9th (which happens to be the story of Noah) along with the accompanying *haftarah* from the prophet Isaiah. Both selections emphasize that God will not let his people down. I try to contrast that content with the content from the *New York Times* in the same time period which speaks of bloodshed, starvation, fierce battles, revolution, counter revolution, peasant uprisings, peasant repression — all in the Province of Kiev where Manya and her children are living.

Admittedly, our Eli is more likely to be reading the Yiddish newspaper, The *Forward*. But news is news and the headlines in the *New York Times* in September/October 1918 are full of threat, darkness, intrigue. *South Ukraine in Revolt. German Mutineers Join Ukraine Rebels. Ukraine Aflame Against Germans.* Reading further . . . *The population of Kiev is starving. Unrest among the peasants is spreading. German mutineers join peasants with fierce fighting and many losses. Austrians proclaim a state of siege in Odessa and order the people of Odessa not to join in the revolutionary movement.*

On October 9, 1918 Eli pens a beautiful letter to his son.

To my dear son Benyamin, may his light shine.

> *My dear Benyainka the small one, you must be asking yourself the question, why is it that you have to grow up without a Father. The answer is that is the will of God. This answer may satisfy you but to me things are very bad and I owe a debt which has to be repaid. But my dear child do not ask questions. I ask you my son, the little one, with all your strength that you honor your mother and protect her with all your strength and do so by being a straight boy and a true man in your relations to both God and your fellow men. My dear son Benyamin let it be so that we have a world free from violence and that I shall see you. And so I grab a moment now to write you this letter for at present who knows what tomorrow will bring. Be healthy and with joy and be a Jew with all your heart. May God help you. From your Father who kisses you; I hold you close to my heart.*
>
> *Eliyah.*

My father was eight years old when he received that letter. Four more years would yet have to pass before their separation was over. My father kept this letter with him through those years, packed it with his belongings on the sea voyage to America. I wonder did he ever take it out to look at it over again. Despite the sentences penned by Eli's children for their wishes to reunite, I wonder how, when father and son did reconnect, how their reunion went. You see my father had only just turned twelve at that point. When I asked, my father answered: "Our relationship was cool." I suppose the eight-year separation—the extraordinary difference in experience—was not easy to bridge. More to the point, Eli may well not have understood my father, the *artiste*. Eli, the businessman, surely concentrated on getting his oldest son Oscar established in his line of work, enabling him to eventually take over Eli's dry goods store. Eli could ignore his youngest child who still had some years ahead of him, and who, perhaps, Eli saw as only wanting to read, write and draw.

One hundred years later I am reading Eli's instructions to his son, my father. And I think . . . I have been a non-religious, secular Jew. Yes, my children went to Sunday School. My daughter had her *Bat Mitzvah*. My son, his *Bar Mitzvah*. Up on the *bimah* two times, I faced each child with motherly pride and spoke about passing to them the responsibility to be a *link in the unbroken chain of Jewish tradition*. But I was separate; not a believer, not someone who actively practiced the Jewish faith. I did not know the word *faith*. I did not consider much my relations with God. I did not know what Eli meant to "be a Jew with joy and with all your heart." And neither of my marriage partners—the fathers of my children—were Jews.

On one occasion before one of my business trips to Russia my father suggested I try to find a copy of Isaac Babel's stories. "He wrote in Russian, you know, *Boobala*, not Yiddish. Yet he writes about our seed. You will read his stories for yourself. Read *The Story of My Dovecote*." My "seed" . . . that didn't register. Nothing registered. Yet here I was, far from my seed. Very far.

From Manya's letters, spiritual matters—faith and God's will—were very much a part of her life. Faith and Hope. Would any of this Jewish faith have helped me? Helped my angry and joyless marriage?

I needed a different structure in order to thrive—not a stultifying home of depression but a home where life was good. I needed, but I couldn't ask for, this. I doubt I could really see what I needed because I couldn't feel that my sacred self deserved to be honored. I couldn't see that I am a deserving soul. I saw squeezing my "stuff" in surreptitiously. Under cover. Squeezing me in under cover. Or under a cloud of anger. I couldn't say, W*e are not living a life that a life deserves. We are settling for too little. For much too little.* I couldn't see a way out. I couldn't see to ask for help. I couldn't see that *suffocation of the spirit* is the loss. I could be angry but I could not be compassionate. I didn't know. I didn't understand from where my anger, my pain was coming. The pain of my mother and father (my experience of their struggle) had been buried now for years. I couldn't see my life was taking on the color of their life. I couldn't see through the layers of cover-up, not then. And I couldn't talk to God about this. I could only ask questions.

My soul needed to thrive but who am I to ask that?

Who am I to seek to order my life in such a way as to satisfy my soul?

To whom am I responsible once I have chosen to have children?

Is this the ultimate question in this, our one and only journey?

Does the soul have to shrivel?

To what are we beholden?

To whom are we beholden?

Before whom do I stand?

Is it really true that what I want for myself, and what God wants for me, might be the same thing?

Is my contract with God that I honor my creativity and create?

I make one marriage that is not a good marriage. We have one child, my daughter Rachael. But this marriage is very bad. I must walk away. I walk away with my one-year old daughter. We are in Cameroun, West Africa in the Peace Corps, and I walk away. I am not a coward. I had the certainty that this was right regardless of how it would turn out. I *knew* this was the right thing to do. I kept my integrity.

My second marriage is also not a good marriage. But one that is not so egregiously wrong that I must walk away. A marriage with some benefits. We have one child, my son Amos. And this time I *am* a coward. I *know* this is not right but I stay. I stay in a wrong marriage.

How much is lost when soul shrivels?
This husband allowed me my career.
This depressed man.
He does not count? He ought to count.

Are there no answers?
There are no answers.
Children are affected.
Finally I ask him to walk away.
He walks away.

Souls ask to live. My soul wants to live.
How much is gained when souls thrive.

And so our journeys are what?
To keep swimming up the stream?

Souls ask to live. My soul wants to live.
How much is gained when souls thrive.
And didn't my father speak this? Even if in silence, to my mother?
Didn't my mother speak this? Even if in silence, to my father?
Didn't my father need his soul to live?
Didn't my mother need her soul to live?
And didn't I need my soul to live?

In whose presence am I?

Help. Salvation. Compassion. Trust. A willingness to surrender. A higher power. The God of my understanding. Repair. All fortunately have come my way. "We must come to these things ourselves, in our own ways," repeating the words of our beloved, retired rabbi. "And it must come in more than words, it must come in actions."

19. RAGAMUFFINS, BAREFOOT, AND HUNGRY

*T*he chaos of family survival—matched up with the chaos of state survival—leave very few options for Manya and her children. Disarray was everywhere and famine was soon to descend. Military fighting was over. Lenin's Bolshevik party had consolidated power. The Red Army—no longer fighting the Poles, nor the Tsarists—had finally gained control over those who sought an independent Ukraine. But the nascent Soviet state—huge and weakened by its efforts to end World War I and then Civil War—nonetheless was fighting for its life, particularly its economic life. Soviet requisition policies, kulak / peasant resistance to those policies, and systemic breakdown of the war-torn transportation system combined with drought to bring famine of unprecedented size to many parts of Russia in 1921, not just the Ukraine.

No wonder that my father writes (later in a reminiscence):

...Hungry children wandering aimlessly on hot city streets. Their eyes, falling on bricks or stones, plead, Why is it not bread? Why so many hard bricks, why so little bread? Here and there lying in gutters, a body with a bloated stomach, a leg already mutilated by dogs. Black heavy flies swarm around new meat.

But now the letters from Manya's family to Eli are straight to the point: Eli's oldest daughter Rivka, now seventeen, writes *"We are ragamuffins, barefoot, and hungry."* Klara, Manya's sister, and her brother Veniamin write about hunger and no money. Mokha writes that after the pogrom of 1920 the family is *"spread everywhere with no way to help each other."* Far flung. Everyone on his/her own. Mokha in Gomel. Klara in Ekaterinoslav. Veniamin and Liuba in Kiev. Manya and kids in Smela, then in Nikolaev.

The first letter Eli receives after a three-year black out is Mokha's.

December 26, 1920

Dear Eli,

Again we try one way or another to give you news of our existence. It has been two years since I tried to send a letter to you via a mission leaving Ukraine for America, but it didn't succeed. I'll keep this short and try to report the situation of your family. One letter by way of [a Jewish organization] we did receive from you last summer, and not long ago we got a postcard. About what has happened, how we have lived up to now, there isn't time to write, but I can tell you about your family's situation now.

After the pogrom in Gorodische this past fall (1920) Manya and the younger children left for Smela, where they now live. Isor and Sonya [Ed: Rivka is also called Sonya] are in Nikolaev; Meer is serving in the military, we think in Kremenchug. To speak in greater detail how Manya and the children live and on what means, I can't say; it's been a long time since I've been "home" and I write on the basis of what Veniamin (who lives now in Kiev with Liuba) writes me. I am with the Soviet Merchant Marine now. I moved from Kiev to Gomel which is the winter repair station for our ships. I'll be here to Spring. In sum, big changes have happened to our family and we have suffered much loss.

About the death of our father (spring 1918) you no doubt know, but our mother was killed in the pogrom in the Fall of last year (1919) in which our Veniamin also suffered wounds. From the wound in his right arm it was necessary to amputate.

In March I married a Kazanka, whose parents live in America. I'll give you their address but it is old and we haven't heard from them since 1917. . . . Our Klara lives now in Ekaterinoslav, where she works in an apothecary. Your brother Chaim it seems has resettled in Nikolaev.

A little while after the pogrom in Gordische, Liuba's mother died, so her father now lives with her and Veniamin in Kiev. So you see we are now spread far and wide and there is no way and no means to help one another. We await a better future where we can see you or a future where your family sails to America. I would write more but I am not sure this will reach you. I'll write again. Be well. Your Mokha

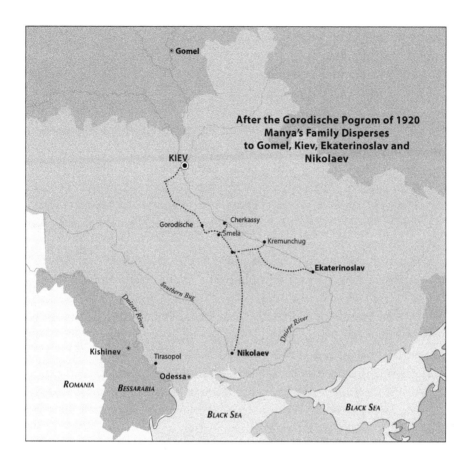

Gomel

After the Gorodische Pogrom of 1920
Manya's Family Disperses
to Gomel, Kiev, Ekaterinoslav and
Nikolaev

KIEV

Cherkassy
Gorodische
Smela
Kremunchug
Ekaterinoslav

Southern Bug

Dniestr River

Dnieper River

Kishinev
Tirasopol
Nikolaev
Odessa
ROMANIA   BESSARABIA

BLACK SEA

BLACK SEA

Yes, everyone *was* on their own. The tight-knit, managing-rather-well family our wheeler-dealer Mokha had cared for in Gorodische was no more. The pogrom of 1920 finished that chapter of their lives. Far flung, they were. Klara in Ekaterinoslav, Mokha (now a member of the Communist Party) with his new wife in Gomel, Beniamin and Liuba in Kiev. And Manya, first with her in-laws in Smela, then with relatives in Nikolaev (near Odessa). Indeed, no one could help each other very much. The devastation, especially as the summer arrives and the great famine of 1921-22 descends, was widespread and everywhere.

Meanwhile the children write at Passover, 1921:

Rivka (now 17) writes: *Tomorrow is Pesach. We are like foreigners in a foreign land. We are wanderers, ragamuffins, barefoot. It's enough. Bring us to you.*

125

And Iosif (now 13): *It has been seven years since we have seen you. The seventh Passover since we sat with you for Seder. Bring us to you.*

And Niuma (my father, now 11): *When are you going to come and get us? It's enough now being without you.*

The children's Aunt Klara is also blunt: *We are in need of every item for life's necessities. We are without shelter, clothing. We have become very poor . . . .*

Again, Rivka: *Don't waste time. Send money. Do what is needed, not what you can. You are in a good country and have it better than us. Pay attention! We have no more strength nor resources to live this way. . . No, father. I hide nothing. If you knew we unfortunates, you wouldn't sit as you are.*

But Rivka is wrong. Eli and his brother Meir Ben-Ami in Eretz Yisrael are working to make a plan, *even as this news cannot soothe the family for they have no notion of it yet.*

By the month of May 1921, after Passover, Manya has received news of the plan conceived by Meir Ben-Ami. In a letter to Eli dated March 1921, Meir Ben-Ami writes: *If Mali [this is a short form for Manya] can cross the Russian border into Bessarabia, she will find documents at the British Embassy there permitting her to travel to Israel.* Bessarabia is the closest state across the border from Nikolaev and accessible by train from Odessa. A disputed territory between Russia and Rumania, Bessarabia became an independent state in 1921. The capital of Bessarabia was Kishinev.

Meir Ben-Ami continues:

I have sent letters for Mali to Lemberg [then Poland, renamed Lvov] to a certain man and he in turn will forward them to Russia. It is my great hope that they will receive the letters and so is my great expectation that I'll receive letters from them. I also sent Mali documents issued by the government of Eretz Yisrael [Palestine] addressed to the British consul in Warsaw, Poland and to the consul in Kishinev, Bessarabia which will allow her to come to Eretz Yisrael.

If she will succeed to cross the border to get to Kishinev then she will find right away a document at the British consulate which will allow her with ease to come to Eretz Yisrael. I wrote to her that if she succeeds in crossing the border (many people do so) then she should let me know right away and then either I will go there so as to take her to Eretz Yisrael or I'll send her money. From Eretz Yisrael she will be able to travel to you.

I also sent documents for our mother if she is at present alive. In these documents I took it upon myself to support her for one year. It is obvious that this is not within my ability but at present I am not thinking about this, the main thing is to take them out of that geheynom [hell] and to save their lives.

Your brother Meir Ben-Ami

Isor is now aware of this plan and writes to his father from Kiev.

May 8, 1921

Dear Papa,

Uncle Meir in Palestine writes that as soon as he receives a letter from us he will send permissions and money for our journey to Palestine and from there to America.

With great impatience we await that happy moment when we will have received what is needed to leave. In your letter which you didn't date (it's absolutely necessary to date) you wrote that you sent 10,000 rubles but we haven't received them and I don't know whether we will or will not. Generally there is talk and I too understand that relations with America are not yet regular enough especially in the exchange of currencies.

That we first go to Palestine is good. Being in Palestine will make it easier and quicker to get the necessary permissions, letters and money to be able to come to America.

Dear Papa! How happy we would be to leave here this summer, so therefore don't hesitate one second. Do what is needed with Uncle so we can leave.

I leave further details about us for the time when we are all together again. Being together again is our singular hope. Isor

Later he adds with his goodness and compassion: *If it is possible it would be desirable that Aunt Klara, and Uncle Veniamin with his wife Liuba could also come to America but I don't know if Uncle Veniamin would be allowed now, as he is an invalid without an arm.*

Besides writing to his father in America, Isor writes as well to his Uncle Meir Ben-Ami in Eretz Yisrael on the same date.

May 8, 1921

> *Dear Uncle,*
>
> *I have once already written that we received your letter dated 12th of January. You addressed it to us in Gorodische not knowing that we have been living in Nikolaev. Your letter was relayed to us by friends so please in the future write to us in Nikolaev (Rybnaya Street care of B Brodianskii, for Manya).*
>
> *Dear Uncle, I am sure that Yakov, the son of Aunt Yakhna, has already told you about the details of our wretched existence. And therefore I am guessing you, not waiting to receive any letters from us, will be sending the permissions and money. Although money transfers (which of course we very much need) are rather risky now, I don't know for sure but that's what I have heard. Still if you can send the money with a guarantee that it will arrive, do so.*
>
> *In a word, do all that you think you need to because our fate is in your hands right now. I beg you don't hesitate not a second to send all that we need to leave here for Palestine without problems. Uncle Yudil and Aunt Yakhna soon will be leaving. . . . I am living with the hope that soon we will be with you, Isor.*

Isor is right. Sending money doesn't work. *You wrote that you sent 10,000 rubles, but we haven't received them and I don't know whether we will or we will not.* The USA had no diplomatic relations with the nascent Soviet state. There were no legal channels for money transfers in 1921. Any attempt on Eli's part to send money this way was chimerical. America saw the Bolsheviks as its enemy, intervening against the Bolshevik regime. Diplomatic relations between USSR and the USA weren't established until 1933! This is eleven years *after* the USSR was officially formed in Dec 1922 at a conference joining the Russian RSFSR with the Belorussian SFSR, the Transcaucasian SFSR, and the Ukrainian SSR.

Note the devalued ruble. Instead of the usual 100 rubles Eli used to send periodically to his family, costing him $40 each time, the amount that Eli has said he sent is now *one hundred times* the old amounts, or 10,000 rubles. It appears his forty dollars can get 100 times what it used to in terms of rubles. The ruble is cheap against the dollar now. The value of the ruble (in terms of how much holders of dollars will pay for it) has collapsed. And will devalue even further. Unfortunately, buying rubles with dollars now officially in 1921 is impossible; there are no official legal channels. Only black markets.

Troubles and anxieties. Long gaps in communication between Manya's family in Russia, Eli in America and Meir Ben-Ami in Eretz Yisrael cause much anxiety, uncertainty and confusion. Letters that never arrive. Money sent that disappears. Letters that get sent to the wrong address. Some letters do reach their destination but these take a minimum of one month and, oftentimes, much longer. So we are in the catastrophic space where letters cross, and nothing can be confirmed. Yet time and suffering continues.

Weeks go by, months go by without resolution. Isor shows his distress.

May 30, 1921

Dear Papa,

It's been almost two months since we received your last letter and about one month ago we got a letter forwarded to us from Gorodische from Meir in Palestine in which he writes for us to send him immediately our address so he can send money and permissions for our travel to Palestine and from there to America.

Dear Papa! It is very difficult for our family now without you. All of us, but especially Mama and the children are suffering greatly. Life is very difficult. We are all like beggars and often hungry. In my previous letters I wrote very little about all this and this time

I will also write very little because I can't and because it is sure to distress you.

You mustn't wait even a second but do all that is possible yourself or through Uncle Meir so that we receive what we need to leave here. The history of our trials and tribulations over the last years is painful and there is much suffering. To describe it isn't worth the ink on this paper. But everything that has happened we can talk about when we are all together again.

What's singularly important now is that you take all the necessary measures without delay needed for our leaving. All of us greet you. Mokha has a son, Lev, named after grandfather. Be well, I wish you success.

Your son,

Isor

Now communications break down again. Here is Eli's brother, Meir Ben-Ami, in a letter dated Third *Tammuz* (sometime in June 1921) writing to Eli from Palestine:

Three months have passed since I got a letter from you and this surprises me greatly. Why do you not let me know if your family has come to you or did not. A week ago Yudil and Yakhna came to me. They came totally impoverished. They were robbed on the border. They are old and weak. Though Yudil says that he has come to Eretz Yisrael to work, to haul stones, etc., the truth is that he cannot perform any work.

. . . If members of your family did arrive then do give them my regards. The poor wretches. How much did they suffer — that is the question.

Be in peace, Your brother M. Ben-Ami

Our mother, may she rest in peace, died on the 17th of Adar, 1921.

More time goes by without resolution. Isor is persistent.

July 22, 1921

Dear Papa,

We are getting letters from you except that you are addressing them to Gorodische, from which we left after the last pogrom. We are living in Nikolaev, so please write and address your letters to Nikolaev [address here].

About our life I would like to write and write but I don't want to darken your life. I will say only that we have lived through much suffering and God only knows what's ahead. Details of our family life and my life are really awful and with difficulty somehow we are living through this.

According to you we were supposed to receive from Masterov 10,000 rubles, 40 dollars. But no Masterov. It seems he has returned to America, he already was in Nikolaev and decided not to go to Gorodische. From Uncle Meir in Palestine we have received a letter in which he says if we send him our address he will send money and permissions for us to travel to Palestine and from there to America.

I have written him several letters without any answer back. Many people are leaving Russia for America. Uncle Yudil and Aunt Yakhna have left for Palestine. We are here waiting. I'd like to write and write but I only say a little and certainly not enough. We will leave all that for the time when we can be together. Do everything possible so that we can get out of here or else you come here. Write to our address in Nikolaev.

Your son,

Isor

Again, we read: *I would like to write and write but I don't want to darken your life.* Although Isor and Manya conceal the details of their situations, times have worsened. The Great Famine of 1921 has descended. I find the details in the reports and records of the American Relief Administration (ARA). The U.S. Congress in 1921 created the

ARA to provide food relief for those starving in Russia. Initially focused on the Volga River Valley, the ARA found conditions in the Ukraine as serious as any in the Volga Basin and thus expanded its operations to the Southern Ukraine. One of the districts included in the ARA's food relief operation was the Nikolaev district.

Nikolaev — where Manya and her family lived, embedded with Eli's relatives.

Based on reports of the ARA and of the European High Commissariat of Dr. Fridtj Nansen, the famine of 1921 was the worst in Russian history to date (until the Ukrainian famine of 1930). The 1921 famine was a result of bad weather combined with the effects of the Great War, in which "eleven million men and two million horses" were taken from the countryside for the war effort decimating the agricultural work force. Add to this the harsh policies of Lenin's "War Communism" — requisition and confiscation — which resulted in a fierce backlash from protesting peasants now back from the war. The result was a reduction of land cultivation to a bare minimum. And a crisis of unprecedented proportions. Massive suffering, starvation, death, disease.

For the people of the Nikolaev district, and of course for Manya and her children, the Great Famine presented the last in a chain of disasters. To repeat: the turmoil and chaos of Revolution, Civil War, World War I, and drought. Four years of civil war and foreign intervention had devastated the land. Contending forces had requisitioned or confiscated almost all the grain, horses, and livestock. The drought of 1921 compounded the calamity by destroying that grain which had been sown.

Isor and Manya mention their plight but it is quickly cut short by sentences like: *We will wait until we see you,* or: *In my previous letters I wrote very little about all this and I will also write very little now . . . because it is sure to distress you.* Only Rivka shows us the intensity of her emotions and the family's fragile state in a torn fragment from that time. She admonishes her father for not helping them in their dire state. She is crying tears as she writes. She cannot believe his attitude that to her appears indifferent and unconcerned. She writes her family is worn thin, barefoot, yet he doesn't seem to understand their suffering. *How cold and official your letters seem. You seem to think we are doing okay.*

132

How wrong you are, father. If you understood our suffering, how much we have suffered, you would never write as you do. I never expected this from you.

In a letter to her uncle, she appeals for his help.

September 5, 1921

Dear Uncle,

Your letter how fast it gets here! As far as us getting to America nothing new has happened. We have to get into this deeper. It appears as if Papa isn't aware how we are living and suffering, what we have been through for the last seven years. It seems as if it's all the same to him. We got a letter from him on the 17th of July where he writes that he can't do anything more for us. That's our father!!

You can imagine how painful it is for us to hear such words. We already don't have the strength to keep going, there is nothing to live for except to leave here. We are barefoot . . . We haven't see my brother Meer for two years. Isor at the moment is away at work.

Many people here are being sent packages and money, but it seems our father is not taking such measures for us. We sit here . . .

Riva

20. WHEN THE RIVER ICE FLOWS

*T*he congratulatory, celebratory dinner party my colleagues had for me had long faded. The recognizable honor of being the first researcher allowed in the Russian Far East under the US-USSR Bilateral Exchange agreement wasn't enough to trump the objections of my husband. The tension and near breaking point of my marriage were the overwhelming threat. But, yes, the flight to Tokyo was to leave on schedule, and I was determined to be on it. The consequences were enormous. Dark waters where dolphin and whales heed each other's calls, but where for us, when we call, there is no one.

Papa! Papa! The children from Gorodische cry. Come! Help!

Momma! My 12-year old son calls. Come! Help!

I didn't hear. I wasn't there. I never saw the blood. I was far away. I never understood his terror. I never knew his fear. "I remember the day," he tells me 30 years later, "Dad and I were playing basketball. Dad was trying to pay more attention to me I think because you weren't there. I went inside to go to the toilet and I was bleeding. I was so scared. And you weren't there."

I never saw it. Is it like the blood after birth? Is it like menstrual blood? No I was not there. To hold my son. To comfort him. I was not there. To assure him.

"But you are here now Mom." My son and I have just had a meditation sit together and he can tell me in a remarkably calm voice (a voice that comes from the peaceful place a meditation practice can provide) that from a trip to South America he has caught a vicious bacterial illness, his digestive system is again compromised and he is understandably afraid. Afraid that he will bleed again. But this time I can listen for I am equally calm and I can see *for the first time*.

That's right, they couldn't even call me. That time, thirty years before, a telegram from them would always get to me, but not phone calls. Calls took know-how, took practice, took luck. The time difference always at issue. (Calling from Seattle, the time in Khabarovsk was six hours earlier in the next day.) There was no spontaneity possible. Impossible to say "Let's call Mom right now."

Amos, I want to say, *the Friday night I arrived in Khabarovsk I attempted to phone you. The time differences meant that were I to catch you before school — let's say between seven and eight in the morning — I would have to call at one a.m. in the morning my time. But ordering a call doesn't mean getting a call through. First, I must call the international operator an hour before I want to be connected. If I want to reach you at 8 am, then I call the operator at 1 am to put in my request. Then I stay up worrying at that wee hour, Will she call me back as I have asked. But she does, "We will try to connect with America now." That would be fine if the call would go through as ordered. But the call might not connect, then the operator would say, "I cannot get through, shall I try again in twenty minutes?" And then the same thing again, sometimes two more times, until finally the window of opportunity would close: you kids would have left for school.*

That phone call I made the night I arrived did go through but only to demonstrate another set of difficulties between us. I could hear you but you couldn't hear me. There was nothing to be done. A request to call America does not mean a connection. A connection does not mean a two-way connection.

"Why did you go without us? Why didn't we all go together? Why did we have to split up? Why didn't you want us with you?" you might ask me now. Amos, I answer, your father and I did deliberate should you go with me. The authorities nixed it, saying they couldn't take on the responsibility. And yes, I was conflicted. I would have loved having you with me even though I knew I wouldn't have been able to focus as well on my work.

Exactly three weeks after I arrived in Khabarovsk, you and your father arrived for a one-week visit. We had planned this, tickets had been bought before I left. Your sister Rachael, a sophomore in high school with boys on her mind, had decided to pass on this trip. (Remember Chuck was her stepfather. The connection between them vastly more distant than for you.) I expected that a visit from you would help the feeling of my "awayness." I know I left you all very unhappy. You said, "Don't go. You can cancel." Your sister said straight out, "Mom I am not coping. What if Aimée dies, if you die, if Amos dies. Mom, I am having a nervous breakdown." In reality, your father was having the nervous breakdown though not able to say those words directly.

The morning of my departure you and your father were getting ready to take me to the airport. You came out of the bathroom saying, "Mom, I have diarrhea." My mind was elsewhere. I would not see beneath your statement. Nor would I have been able to do anything about it. I was set to go. The flight, a non-stop to Tokyo, was waiting.

The Institute of Economic Research where I was to be a guest was in Khabarovsk, a city on the Amur River. The best route at that time to my destination Khabarovsk was to fly via Japan: to Tokyo, then via train to Niigata, a small city on Japan's Honshu Island's northwest coast where once a week, every Friday morning, a flight left for Khabarovsk. Niigata is a two or three hour train ride from Tokyo's Narita airport. The trip therefore requires an overnight in Niigata. That was the way I arrived and that is how son Amos and husband Chuck would come. One could go to Khabarovsk via a *daily* flight from Moscow but that would mean going *east* from Seattle over the pole to Moscow, then east again across the great land mass of Russia—traversing in total two continents and the Atlantic Ocean. Going *west* from Seattle to Khabarovsk meant crossing the Pacific to Japan, and a short hop across the Sea of Japan to Russia's far eastern territory.

My hotel room window faced the Amur River. The Amur is one of the ten largest rivers in the world and forms a border between Russia and China. This important river brags the largest fresh water fish in the world, the Kaluga carp. The Kaluga carp (a relative of the Beluga carp) can reach to one ton in weight, and 18 feet in length, and live as many as 55 years. It devours everything. It is second only to the Beluga in terms of the quality of its roe.

What was I thinking? I could go away for three months without impunity? That Chuck could handle it? Well . . . you were coming. You would see where I stay, the city I am living in. The river I talk about. We'd continue by letters, by telephone. That's what I was thinking.

The discouragement, frustration, sadness of not communicating on that first phone call when I could hear my children's voices but they couldn't hear me. . . all that evaporated when I turned to the world at hand. My proposed work at the Institute for sure. But to my surprise, the frozen river. It fascinated me. At that month of March, it was in its solidly frozen state, bustling with activity: trucks criss-crossing the river, folks walking, fishermen fishing through ice-holes. A New England pond for ice-skating had been my only previous winter-ice experience. I was eager to walk across that river following what it seemed other people were doing. And so just two days after my arrival, on a Sunday bright, with sky clear and blue, I thought to try. Yet, just a few steps out, I knew immediately I wasn't dressed nearly warmly enough. Much, much too cold. I'd have to come back another time, with warmer clothes on. A time soon, I said to myself, before the ice becomes too thin.

I kept a journal on this trip. For each day I made four columns: the new Russian words and phrases I had learned; the day's doings (people, places, calls); the river's status; and notes to myself (various observations of this and that). It took me a couple of weeks before I began to understand about this frozen river and began to note the daily newspaper reports on the "level" of the river. For several weeks straight, the newspaper reports stated "the level of the Amur River (flowing water) was at minus 150 centimeters." So I began to understand, there was river flowing beneath the 1.5 meters of ice, beneath the approximate 5 feet of ice. And while no whales or dolphin were there, the Kaluga was.

We will walk the frozen river together, I said to myself, anticipating naively, nonchalantly, your arrival from Japan. You and your Dad had made it to Japan, you were in Niigata and were awaiting the Friday flight. We will have one week together: Friday to Friday. That will be nice, I say to myself. Yes! We will walk the frozen river together. There would be plenty of time before the ice would become unstable and unsafe, time before the ledokhod. *"There will be plenty of noise," Olga tells me, "you will know. We are given lots of warning," she adds. "When the ice is no longer safe, the ice roads are closed. Warnings are posted. There is lots of time." I was happy, nonchalant and thrilled to be anticipating your arrival and to be planning our walk on the Amur River together. I did not expect to see you so sick and to experience Chuck so weak. You so gaunt, so pallid, so sallow, bone thin. And I had forgotten, or had always been oblivious, to Chuck's tears.*

Your diarrhea was so severe. What would you eat that wouldn't instantly mean a run to the bathroom. I was not kind. I was not compassionate: "You are spoiling everything," I told your father. "You have not been coping." No, Chuck would have said, No, wife, I cannot cope.

I could not understand. He sits on the windowsill of the hotel room and writes his endless notes. No different than at home, sitting in the god-awful corner window nook of our bedroom writing notes on little pieces of paper. Some habit the therapist of his recommends. He is telling me he cannot keep it together. He thinks I will abandon him? He thinks he will be abandoned? His fears coming from some dark very dark interior of his childhood. His frailty spills over us all. I flail at it. Turn away from it. I am cut to the bone. I did not want to see and did not want to hear.

And so after a week of torture—knowing I am helpless because you will go home and I will be staying longer—we say goodbye. You did not beg me to come home, Amos. Thank you, that you did not beg.

Thank you, that you did not beg. That would've been too much for me to bear. You see my father left us, his children, we three, my brother, my sister, me when I also was a young child. I could not, would not beg him to stay. Not one of us three children *showed* emotion. We would not, could not. This is what children do, we are helpless, tongue-tied. We stay silent. We go outside and "play." Hurt hidden until now. Buried until now. Besides I was siding with my mother.

During the separation when we lived in Bethesda, Maryland and my father in Washington DC, my mother told me one evening that my father was coming to visit with her. For "conversation" with her. And that if I should hear him hitting her, I should call the police. I called the police. I knew nothing. I was simply terrified by her suggestion. Except for that action and remembering my brother shivering behind the upstairs door alongside me these matters until now have been long covered over. I have no recollection of any conversation about the trauma that was happening within my family. I only recall a span of time during their separation when I was sure there was someone outside our house just below my second-floor window, digging. Every night I would hear the same digging sound. It so frightened me. I am only now, just now, right now, acknowledging the hurt I felt when our father left us. Yes, my father abandoned us . . . me. I was 10 years old. My brother was seven. My older sister 14. Yes, my father abandoned me, and although I never have put it that way until now, I am putting it that way now. And maybe, just maybe, that was the beginning of when I abandoned part of myself.

And now I was abandoning Amos.

I needed to stay longer in Khabarovsk because—like my mother's intentions and ambitions to do right work, I *was* doing right work, good work, important work and—unlike her, I would not abandon it so quickly.

It never occurred to me to get the next available flight home. I was numb. Paralyzed. Could anyone fathom matters so deep? Only the river to which I turned again and again.

"It's not only the Amur that will deliver its ice to the sea," Alexander tells me, "but the Ussuri River too which flows into the Amur right here in Khabarovsk. The *ledokhod* (the going of the ice) is about eighteen days away."

"How do you know," I ask, "when it will happen?"

"The level of the water will rise. There is fierce wind, loud noise. You will see."

We never got a chance to walk the river. Amos was too sick. I was too angry. I felt the massive calamity at home; that Chuck would be

sitting in corners by windows day after day not getting better. Only introspection, no going forward. Immobility. I ward off my upset before it devours me.

The day after their plane left is a Saturday, April 2, and Passover. I cannot find a Passover Seder anywhere even though I gently, discretely, ask around. Even as I ask about Easter Sunday the replies are muted. This was still the USSR where religion was off-limits: private, hidden, spoken about in whispers. Passover that year was the first ever I have missed in all my years of memory. So I take a walk into the frozen Amur River instead. *For us, Amos. For us.*

I dressed as warmly as I could, and after no more than maybe twenty steps, or half a block I see the reality of what a walk entails. Nothing like I imagined. No smooth, even-if-slippery, paths, nothing like a New England ice-skating pond. This ice-terrain was a complete sea of frozen waves. Three-foot-high frozen waves. Walking up and over or around these was tiring at best. I didn't get that far in the direction of the other side. Still something adhered me to this river. Knowing about the flowing water five feet under the ice. And rising. Are there possibly kindnesses there, compassion? I wanted to befriend this river. Naively for sure but necessary for me. I needed the kindness the compassion too.

No, I didn't book the next available flight home. Rachael and I talked on the phone a few days later. A long clear call from Rachael that Chuck had set up. She sounded very sad. She tells me she is worried. I say (was it to myself or to her?) I will come home if I need to. It's okay I say to her, I have decided I will come home if it is so deemed. That same evening I call Chuck, who says don't worry. So . . . I drop the idea for the moment. I read that the river is rising. It is at minus 104 centimeters. They keep telling me watch for the wind. I am thinking I should go home.

No, I did not book the next available flight home, nor did I book the flight after that one. Even after Chuck's call on April 10th raising the issue of calling me home. Was he really expecting I'd pack up, throw in the towel that fast? On April 10th the radio reports, the level of the river is now minus 94 cm. I want the river ice to go before I have to go. I want to see it, feel it. It will be around the 19th or so of April, my friends tell me.

140

How do they know exactly? Were there rituals in the days of yore by the natives during this moment? I wonder now about this. The indigenous *Evenki* (or Northern *Tungus*) peoples lived along the Amur. Surely something. Celebrations? Rituals? Sacrifices? Supplications? After all, this event is of major proportions. The winter is over! I read now that one such native group, the *Ket* people, invoked their spirit-gods and their spirit-gods' children to speed the breakup of the great Yenisei River's ice. They believe their gods' invisible children were taught to swim under the ice and split it from below with their pointed heads. Offerings of cloth, ribbons, or coins placed on their heads.

Chuck calls again, four days after his last call, on April 14th, telling me Amos is having tests in the hospital. IT'S TIME TO COME HOME, he states unequivocally. Perhaps these were the words of his therapist but certainly in our son's best interests. Yes, I said. OK, I will start the process and plan to come either on one of the next two Fridays— that meant in one or two weeks. I telex my authorizing governmental agency, I have a sick child, I must go home. I tell Chuck to send me a telegram for official purposes to the effect that I am being called home due to my child's severe illness.

Whose illness was it really? Dad couldn't cope. Mom was absent. And then when the parents are together, they succumb to rage and violent speech. Both are contributing to this illness but only one person bears the physicality of it, carries the physical illness.

FEEL THIS , ELISA, BUT DO NOT JUDGE THIS. Let the ice go first, then go, Elisa. Your father asked your mother to reconcile their differences, to end their separation, to go back together and move from Bethesda where your mother had a job and was so happy. She caved. She left her job, "reconciled" only to learn several years later his request was hollow. Your husband, Elisa, is asking you to go home, to leave your work and your job which gives you so much meaning (and which *will* give you so much meaning), to go home to take care of your son because your husband cannot. Your stakes are high: your work, you, the well-being of your son. It is not just your husband calling you to come home, it is for your son your husband is calling you home. They feel abandoned, yet they are asking you to abandon yourself. These are the stakes, Elisa. FEEL THIS. DO NOT JUDGE. Neither assign guilt, nor assign blame. Just feel it. The river waters beneath the ice are rising, they will help your body feel this. Cowards abandon themselves first. Be brave. Not just for your mother, or your mother's mother, not just for your daughter or for your daughter's daughter, but for yourself. Perhaps, if you are very fortunate, eventually even for your grown-up son.

True, I didn't want to go home before I saw the going of the ice. I would walk each day down to the river and look. I think I am seeing it, the teeny-tiny tinkling of vertical ice sticks breaking away from the shore. No, Elisa, Olga says, See? The middle of the river is still solid. No water is visible. You will know. (*When it is time to go?*)

Chuck calls again three days after his last call. April 16, a Saturday. Amos has a bleeding ulcer. I get a telex from my sponsoring agency; they okay my plan and agree to pay for my trip home. I do not book next Friday's flight for April 22. The newspaper reports *water level of the Amur River is at 0 centimeters. Expected to rise to plus 30-35 cm in the next few days. The ledokhod (the going of the ice) is expected also in the next few days.*

April 19. It's windy which is what Alexander says you need for the ice to move. I thought I was seeing it a few days earlier, when I walked down to the river edge. For at the edge there was water. No ice. But Olga said, "No, you will know the real thing." Nonetheless I liked what I saw. Watching ice beak loose and join the current. The tinkle-tinkle of moving small pieces of ice. Ice in vertical sticks. It's happening, I decide anyway.

April 20. Lots of wind last night. The *ledokhod* is happening!

There is flowing water everywhere and is taking the ice downstream. The water has risen. The river is now water. Flowing. Lots of moving ice. Big blocks of ice, as big as houses, hotels. Castles! Fortresses! Moving out. Fast.

April 22. I do not take the flight to Japan.

April 23/24. The Amur River is flowing very fast now still with lots of ice. All the ice is being emptied into the sea. It's still coming. The ice from the whole Amur and Ussuri Rivers.

April 25. On the radio: *sploshnyi [full] ledokhod, moschnyi [at full power] ledokhod na Amur (on the Amur).*

I didn't take the Friday flight on the 22nd because after Chuck's call I was invited for a first-ever visit to Vladivostok. This was a gift.

A diplomatic breakthrough for Soviet-American academic relations. We would sign an official protocol for mutual cooperation between the Far East Science Center (a branch of the National Academy of Sciences) and the University of Washington, which I represented. Vladivostok had been a closed city since 1974. It is Russia's most important city on its Eastern Coast, host to its Pacific Naval Fleet. Besides its military importance is its many research institutes. But international conferences were always held in the neighboring port town of Nakhodka. Soviet scientists travelled to Nakhodka (via a horrendous potholed, winding, cliffhanger of a road, a two hour drive away) to meet with counterparts. Even the famous Trans-Siberian Railroad, always full of tourists, skipped Vladivostok to stop one station further east, the smaller port city of Nakhodka.

That the Russian National Academy of Sciences' Far Eastern Branch agreed to an official well-publicized visit by an American scholar was an honor as well as historic. The barriers put up during the Cold War were beginning to wobble. On Monday night April 25, Olga, my official guide, and I caught the overnight train to Vladivostok. The minute I stepped from the train in Vladivostok, greeted by these and those various officials, I temporarily lost all thoughts about having to go home. After two full days in Vladivostok, we take the evening train back to Khabarovsk. It is Thursday April 28. The river is transformed! All water. Blue water. Large ships and barges everywhere. Every last piece of ice gone. The river is now completely free. I can see the whole river basin. *You can go home now, Elisa. You did not cave.*

I went to see a movie that night, *Repentance*, and walked back to the hotel at 9:30. I had read and reread Chuck's telegram received before the trip to Vladivostok. I had still not booked the flight for the next day, the 29th. But sometime between walking back from the movie and the next morning I knew I must go home. This is over. I must go home. And so I prepared. Flights out of the Russian Far East to Japan were still only once a week. I had one day to prepare to leave. I prepared. I bought a ticket, I paid my bills. I left my typewriter with its special cyrillic keyboard, my plastic shoes, and a note for the Institute's Director under whose umbrella I had been working. That is all I could do. The desk clerk of the Intourist Hotel where I had been living followed my taxi all the way to the airport to collect a few more kopeks that I had owed. No one came with me to say farewell, although certainly my leaving was known to everyone on whose watch list I was. Certainly they had read the telegram they had handed to me. Or knew about the ticket I had just bought. But I left without a farewell. In two hours I was in Japan. I called home immediately to say I was on my way. I made that Friday-morning flight to Japan. I never did get to walk all the way across the frozen Amur River. Or perhaps I did.

Do I get it now? Yes, when I see spilt blotches of blood that didn't quite get wiped up. Can I really know what this brings back for you? Your traumas during sixth grade. Getting treatment and respite from the symptoms of ulcerative colitis but puffing up like a balloon on the prednisone. Playing baseball with the disability. Do I really understand what it is like to have to run into the bushes because you are bleeding diarrhea and having to wipe with pieces of paper from your homework assignments and then leave the bloody underpant mess in the bushes? Do I get it, even today, what it was like?

Does getting it now compensate for the fact that back then your life was draining from you. That my action to leave come hell or high water when your father was telling me he couldn't cope, what a transgression that was. You took it in the gut. Your mother punched. Your father punched. Does anyone really want to deny this melodrama?

21. Waiting To Leave

*M*anya and Isor never give us the emotionally wrenching picture as Rivka does. But vivid descriptions in the reports of the American staff working for the ARA during 1921 and 1922 in the Nikolaev district tell us a lot. One employee Mayer Raskin was responsible for ARA's food relief efforts in the Nikolaev, Elizavetgrad (now called Kirovograd), and Kherson districts of Southern Ukraine. This area had about a million and a half people; one-third to one-half to two-thirds (depending on which report you read) of the people in dire need.

It is a daily sight to find people dying in the streets from hunger, Raskin reports from the city of Nikolaev to the ARA. *The hospitals are crowded with hunger and typhus victims. The children's institutions are in a deplorable condition and many of them possess a ward set aside for the 'candidates of death'.*

James Hodgson, the ARA supervisor for the neighboring Odessa district, describes the very grave conditions there and in the Nikolaev Districts in his reports to the ARA. *Live skeletons of children and adults in the streets crying out, I want bread! I want to eat! . . . Morgues and trucks are piled high with cadavers, some of which been gnawed by dogs. Due to a breakdown in transportation, the dead sometimes lie in the streets for days or weeks, causing passers-by to flee to the other side of the street. And many of the survivors had reached such a point of physical deterioration that their horrible appearance made others shudder, as they were, so to say, on the verge of death.*

The Great Famine lasted from 1921 through 1922. Colonel William R. Grove who oversaw the operations in these districts found railroad stations overflowing with *a mass of humanity of both sexes and of all ages—all in a fearful state as to clothing and lack of food.* He continues: *After several months of familiarity with the starvation scenes, the outstanding memories are of trainload after trainload of ragged refugees crowded into, under, between and upon box cars; pulling out occasional dead ones at junction points; children separated from parents and man from wife, going they knew not where. Lone boys trudging along the highways or beating their way on the bumpers of railroad cars, going from desolation to try to reach a government or city where they heard there was bread; thousands of these when reduced to exhaustion, seeking refuge in institutions; the terrible sight of hundreds of these children in institutions and hospitals which were without food, where they slowly wasted away and died. The poor, in what were once prosperous peasant villages, digging in the countryside for roots or trying to find seeds in the tumbleweeds of last year, and at last turning back to their homes where other members of the family are dead or dying, realizing fully that unless outside help came the same fate awaited them.[1]*

Manya is desperate, and confused. Referring to the plan from Meir Ben-Ami, she writes to Eli:

July 28, 1921

> *Greatly loved friend Eli,*
>
> *I can write to you that I received from Palestine from Meir a letter he wrote to me that I should see to all the possibilities to travel . . . to Rumania. I don't understand, you know well that my best friend, my father, if he had lived would have done everything he could. You know well that I don't have money. Every moment I wish for death. I don't understand.*
>
> *But Meir Ben-Ami also doesn't understand, and he writes to me that I should see that Yudil helps us. You should know that I have lost touch with Yudil together with Yakhna. I don't know what to start to do. I am a dead man. [sic] Without money, one must die. I don't understand the plans. If it were possible, I would already at once travel ... but we are not good, the children are in bad condition... very difficult. I am terrified. . . .*
>
> *There is not the time to remember but remember that I never wanted you to travel . . . Write me. I don't know what to do about traveling. I wondered from the letter what you had sent, did you send money? I don't have the money, I don't have the letter.*
>
> *A lot of people receive packages and I don't know why am I a sinner in God's eyes. Enough ugliness already from your wife, stay healthy, by God with tears every day we should still live well, the young generation should have it easier.*
>
> *Your friend Mali.*

She also writes to Meir Ben-Ami.

August 21, 1921

> *Nikolaev*
>
> *Brother-in-law Meir,*
>
> *I received a letter in which you write that we go to Rumania or to Poland because no one can send anything to Nikolaev (to help us). Then you say Yudil owes us a favor, but this doesn't really help. Before Passover he left for Ribnits [a city in Bessarabia], then he was here on business in Nikolaev but now I don't know where he went.*
>
> *There isn't enough paper to write about our situation. Sadness without end. I am so squeezed in all aspects, clothing, etc. I ask you my brother-in-law take whatever measures are needed to help us. And please write Eli so he is aware how serious this is. Many husbands are sending to their wives their needs.*
>
> *Seven years I have suffered. And still yet. Perhaps we will be saved, God grant this, as it is time for this to end.*
>
> *Be well,*
>
> *Your Manya*

That Manya is not receiving the money Eli says he sending we know, Isor knows, but Eli himself did not know. Money transfers were not getting through. And trusting someone to hide dollars in a pocket or pant cuff and *then* deliver them is subject to great risk. (Recall that Isor writes his father in July that a Mister Masterov who was supposed to deliver them money is nowhere to be found.)

The situation continued for many more months. Raskin reports in the evening of the day the first barge of rations arrived at Nikolaev in May 1922, children began to form lines; by six o'clock the next morning several thousand had gathered at each of the three kitchens, most having waited all night. The kitchen at Dnieprovsk (Aleshiki, now part of Kherson), on the first day of operation, served 6500 children. However it was one incident which made an indelible impression on Raskin. *I noticed a 15-year old girl with a haunted look crying because the workers would not give her food to take home to her brother. When I accompanied the girl home I found the doors locked. Looking through the window, I viewed a young boy lying dead on the floor. The starving girl was trying to use the card of her little brother who had been lying unburied for three days.*[2]

In the same report, we read about Elizavetgrad, the only city in Raskin's district lacking a child-feeding program, *Raskin on arrival found his worst problem was feeding about five hundred abandoned children who roamed streets. Raskin believed the only way he could properly feed them was to have them taken to an orphanage. Learning that the children's home in Elizavetgrad could accommodate up to one thousand, Raskin asked to examine the facility. Accustomed as he was to scenes of desolation, Raskin found the situation there too 'horrible beyond description.' All the inmates were 'stark naked and dying.'*

* * * * *

So we know what Manya must also have known, what she *must have seen*. What Manya's children knew and *must also have seen*. What my father (then 11 years old) knew and *must have seen*.

* * * * *

August 21, 1921

> *Much beloved friend Eli,*
>
> *I cannot understand why you haven't taken us away from here. The only way for you to understand our wretched life is to write to you about everything. First of all, we hunger to see some mercy for the children. Only we should not sin against God, not even a bent spoon. Often I do such things.*
>
> *I don't understand you with your letter. You wrote me in the letter that you would send the 100. If I send you my address, then you will write to me with some dollars and also some news. I have received a letter from Palestine from Meir that he knows that you sent me a 100 rubles. [Manya is confused here.] Probably you wrote to him that. Now he writes to me that I should travel together with Yudil with Yakhna just like that. It is not possible for him to send me a registered letter with money. He writes I should travel no matter*

what over the Rumanian border and, after arriving, telegram you and he will send me everything that I need.

Can't you understand how desperate this makes me? I don't know what to think. I am here with the three smallest children. What if it's too late? Isor is now in Tolne, he was in Kiev. Because of our soldier son Meer, I don't travel. People told me that he was in Vinnitsiya. Now you can understand how I felt when both Meir and you wrote to me that you have a job, thank God and meanwhile we suffer here terribly without an end.

We are naked, barefoot without a piece of clothing. We are in such a critical situation. I don't know what to do. My heart aches from it. . . . There is no pride, no joy. The money—I don't have 40 and I also don't have a 100. Winter is coming. I wish every day for death but I will not sin against God. The children are in want of a piece of dry bread. I don't even know what you are thinking regarding me and the littlest children. Are you planning to take us away from here at all? Meanwhile, they beg.

Meir Ben-Ami writes that Yudil should lend me a sum of money because it is not possible to send money to Nikolaev. There is no guaranteed delivery. I guess I will write Yudil a letter. . . Who knows if they are as rich as we think they are. I don't know what to think anymore. I am begging you again my friend. . . .

Blessed be God, don't forget us. Summer we sleep on the hall floor but winter... I mean, if you still have any kind of feeling for us... You ask where am I in the world. I sit now and write to you as my heart aches within me. What will become of us? Have mercy on the children.

Our children. To suffer like this! The pain I feel in my heart watching them suffer. I am already abandoned. I beg of you again to think of us. No person can make it through the winter without any clothes, going hungry. God will help us to the new year. I wonder why you have not written to me earlier about the anniversary of my father's death. I am ready for us to go. It is already winter, summer is gone and I have no joy, no pride. Don't forget that winter is coming.

Now, Manya's sister Klara, her brother Veniamin, and his wife Liuba, all tell Eli not to send money, only packages.

August 11, 1921

Greetings dear Eliyah,

Your letter dated 16 of June we received yesterday. You can't imagine how happy we were to get it . . It has been three months since I came to live in Kiev from Ekaterinoslav. We live in poverty in every possible way. I don't work but sell at the market from early morning to late at night I am with every kind of rascal and all. Then there is the peasant with his ready fist. I don't earn even enough for necessities, hence I live at the edge of starving. We need everything especially as winter nears.

. . . Don't send money. Money never arrives. But packages do arrive. Many city folk are receiving packages: clothing, foodstuffs. Your family is in desperate need of clothing and shoes. Send foodstuffs too because we can sell what we can't use. How are our relatives there? How come you don't speak of them when you write. How come they are silent?

Your Meir from Palestine has written to Manya a letter which she sent to us. In it he insists that Manya and the children prepare for their leaving and don't stop, not for any obstacle; but unfortunately we know many examples that these actions are in vain and therefore we must wait although waiting is very hard. Your Klara

September 11, 1921 (Letter from Manya's brother Veniamin in Kiev)

Dear Brother Eli,

Life in Kiev is very difficult. Ever since after Pesach [Passover] I have not been able to engage in my profession [Dentistry]. We cannot find a home. Everything requires enormous amounts of money. It's even more difficult for someone who is an invalid, but does the hungry stomach care about that?

I have had to take an occupation that brings only pennies. You have to be able to place yourself in the marketplace and sell soap (on commission), but I am lousy at this. I cannot make a gain.

I was forced to sell myself to be a night guard at [a Jewish organization], all this in order to eat just one piece of black bread. On top of all that Liuba is very unwell and needs to eat. How can one manage that when everything is so expensive and with such a miserly income.

Of course, one has to pull oneself together and to take courage, and then too, maybe things will get better. If it were not for hope, there would be nothing worthwhile to live for.

. . . It's not worth sending money. It's better to send us packages with clothing, shoes, and soap. This is more useful. As a result of the pogroms we are naked and barefoot. Yet to buy something we need millions. You in America certainly must be able to find these things much less expensive. Whatever you send we'll sell it and from that make money.

Veniamin Polansky

The agency helping with packages—given that money was not getting through—was the All Jewish Public Committee for Relief of Pogrom and War Sufferers, headquartered in New York City. Through this organization one could send packages of various items. And those items could be sold for money; the money needed for buying train tickets, sailing tickets, food, and needed clothing items.

Getting to the British Consulates in Rumania or Poland as his uncle has advised will still be tried by Isor. But given that others are receiving packages, getting packages from Eli becomes all consuming.

Notes

[1] Benjamin Rhodes, "American Relief Operations at Nikolaev, USSR, 1922–1923," *Historian* (August 1929): 616–617.
[2] Rhodes, "American Relief Operations," 619.

22. The *Moloch* of Ambition

My family needed me to be home. And I had come home. But during the two months when I was participating in the US-USSR Senior Scholar Research Exchange, I was able to make fertile connections for future work. And so, during the Summer after that Spring 1988 sojourn, when the State of Alaska sensed an opportunity under a warming USSR-US relationship, I was the one to whom it turned. The state's policy makers were working on initiatives to melt the "ice curtain" via people-to-people exchanges. Yes, I answered, Yes. *Nothing will ever be that hard ever again and all is not lost and Yes, I will help. I would limit my time away in Russia to, at the most, only three weeks at a time. That would be okay. Certainly, that would be okay.*

And so, a pattern developed. It went like this:

I have a trip to Russia's Far East.

This trip will be for 12 days.

I had been home for at least one or two months.

I have checked with my husband who has agreed with my plan.

Amos is playing with his friends somewhere in the neighborhood.

Gotta go find Amos and say goodbye.

Gotta go do this.

I find Amos at the beach with his best buddy Cameron, along with his mom who had agreed to watch them both.

It is summer time.

I'll see you in twelve days, Amos.

OK, Mom.

We hug.

Bye Amos.

Bye Mom.

And then . . . in one extraordinary moment my exoskeleton is ripped away. After which—for another extraordinary moment—I am left exquisitely vulnerable. For just one unbearable moment. And then instantly a new exoskeleton begins to harden as I walk away, find my car for the trip to the airport. It happened just like that each and every time. Exoskeleton ripped away. A moment of intense unbearable vulnerability. Followed by a new skin.

It may seem crazy that I compare that singular set of moments with a spider's molt. But I knew something between Amos and me, in Amos, in me was sacrificed—lost forever—during those moments. And before the soft vulnerability could impose its own grace, showing me a way to express the love that I felt, allowing the words to come to my tongue, the hardening of the new skin was taking effect.

Research shows that spiders and snakes molt in order to grow. That the creatures must shed their skin. I do not know how or if I grew each of these times. It was a habit. It was a pattern. I am only trying to sketch these brief, but unbearable moments.

Eli left Russia and Manya to go to America. Manya suffered. Eli (from a sense of the letters his family replied to) must have been writing about a yearning, and a longing to be with his family. Elisa, his granddaughter, left America and her family to go to Russia. Her husband suffered. Yet Elisa, experiencing sadness, confusion, shame and guilt, showed only anger.

Eli had his Jewish faith. Elisa had not her Jewish faith. True, her daughter had celebrated her *Bat Mitzvah* and her son's *Bar Mitzvah* service was not far away, but her only experience in the temple, for example at High Holy Days, were tears. Not sobs, just a spring of tears quietly pouring down her face. Her daughter on one side, her son on the other, yet alone, without comfort.

I don't know how the tenets or precepts of Judaism would have helped me.

Or whether counsel from a rabbi would have helped us. My non-Jewish partner perhaps could not have understood me. Perhaps too, the fact that my husband was not Jewish prevented me from reaching out to him for solace. Inhibited an honesty. Prevented an understanding. Perhaps my gentile husband couldn't see that living a full life is a command of the Torah, and it is painful to see a life foundering without purpose. *"Everything is foreseen, yet freedom of choice is given; and the world is judged by grace, yet everything is according to the amount of work,"* from the Sayings of Our Fathers, the *Pirke Avot* (a gift from my father). Maybe it was about having to celebrate Christmas and have a Christmas tree with red and green lights. Christmas that meant nothing to me, yet without any way to avoid it. A trivial matter, really, provoking a massive conflagration from me (*anger masking loneliness?*).

After my return from Khabarovsk, I learned that my son was diagnosed with ulcerative colitis: the first doctor saying the only real cure was to cut out that half of the intestine that was inflamed, and be left with a bag for excreting matter. Or continue to swell up on prednisone regimens which however cannot go on indefinitely, and continue to suffer with bouts of bleeding, diarrhea, weakness. All this for a twelve-year old boy becoming a teen-ager and soon-to-be entering high school. My son got the brunt of the storms between his father and me. I believe this. A storm, a dynamic that played itself out in his gut, his body, his psyche, more than in any other one of us.

Was it the *moloch* of ambition that drove me? Or was I playing out the dynamics I experienced in my parents' relationship in some *inverted* way. I say inverted because I was not going to be vulnerable like my mother, who lost purpose, work, and meaning when my father left her. Yet I was punishing my husband wrongly. I became overly self-important (behaving like my father? or insisting, like him, on my need for fulfillment even at the expense of family). Or was I experiencing true purpose? In an inscription to me, in a Russian-language book on Russian-American cooperation in the North Pacific,[1] the author writes *You, Elisa, are one of the heroes in this book*, referring to the work I did helping Alaskan natives and officials make a historic meeting with their Russian native and administrative counterparts. I believe it *was* purpose but the *moloch* was close on the scene for sure as was my parents' drama.

It repeats. I felt the pain of my mother wanting a life she didn't get. My son felt the pain of his father, who was unable to cope with in-capacitating fears never revealed. And Yes, I understood nothing. Yes, I did not want to ask. Yet I had said Yes to this husband, said Yes to having a child from this man, said Yes to this father. And now *son and father* were a couple entwined in each other, entrenched together and alone in a situation the father could not deal with. Yet the two together the only comfort there was. Manya had a whole family supporting her when Eli left for America: brothers, sister, father, in-laws. Each one of her children had five siblings for comfort. Manya suffered from the lack of communication but her large family was with her, supporting her. And she was always greeting the relatives in America with whom Eli was living and who, she assumed, supported him.

Why couldn't my husband be strong? I try now, years later, to parse my anger. How helpless I felt. Sadness, Confusion, Guilt. Guilt because in the face of need, I walked away. In the face of mental illness, I turned away. In the face of depression, I poked, belittled, mocked . . . raged. Guilt, too, at the joy of my work. So much guilt: just easier to hide the joy, the celebration, the successes. Let him sit in his chair and do nothing. Let him sit on the couch and watch the TV and do nothing. The anger masked sadness, confusion, guilt, and my personal elation.

Beset by a problem I could not solve, I would ask myself over and over: What am I supposed to do? My work was in every way reaching deep into meaning: combining a purposefulness with certain skills and talents, everyway challenging, everyway rewarding, everyway encouraging, stimulating, satisfying. Did he not understand? I couldn't honor his request to sit and watch TV together. I felt as if I would be sinking into his world. What, exactly, was he asking me? To give it up? To forfeit my life? Yes, it felt like that. Why did it feel like that? Why was I so threatened by his illness, his incapacity to use the life he was given, to honor the gift of life? What was I supposed to do?

If a counselor, a rabbi, anyone, had said before I left on that very first research exchange, Elisa, can you put aside your career aims (especially the travel requirements) for now in order to save your marriage, I would have answered: Salvage a marriage already being ripped to shreds by my anger? By my lack of respect for the vulnerable and fragile husband I had agreed to marry? No, I said, No. I could not. It felt like a no-win situation. I did not want to be like my mother. I would rather be like my father.

The thought of giving up my life—a life of meaning, of purpose, of active engagement, of excitement, of successes—was intolerable. (I would not take on the tragedy of my mother.) It was a zero-sum choice, as I perceived it, I would not survive. Anger masked the fear that I might drown were I to choose to accept the fact that my husband could not cope, and that it was for me to retake the role of family-care. Pointing a finger at my husband, as if to say he is the problem, felt shameful for I knew I was not blame-free. I am not blame-free. Yet acknowledging his depression, acknowledging depression as a mental illness, acknowledging my part in our troubles, felt shameful. I did not know what to do and could not acknowledge the severity of our problems.

How would it be now? Instead of anger I believe I would try to enter into the feelings, accept the drama no longer buried, bring the complexity to the surface, let it breathe the healing air. What complexity? That ideally all souls want to thrive. All souls deserve to thrive and for one to thrive at another's expense is a heavy cost to bear.

Notes

[1] V. B. Timakov and R. A. Bikmuhametov, *Arkticheskie Seyostry, ili Liniya Peremeny* [Arctic sisters, or International Date Line] (Magadan, Russia: Magadanskoye Knizhnoe Izdatel'stvo, 1990), 70–71.

23. In Riga, at Last

We last left Manya desperate for some kind of sign that help from Eli was on the way. But neither packages, nor monies, arrived. So much conflicting and confusing information from Eli's brother in Palestine and from Eli himself. Six months had passed since Meir Ben-Ami's wrote his letter to Manya that once she is across the border either to Kishinev (Bessarabia) or Warsaw (Poland) she will find papers at the British Embassy allowing her to travel and he will send her money to get to Eretz Yisrael. Isor replies to this plan.

October 6, 1921

> *Nikolaev*
>
> *Dear Papa,*
>
> *Today we received from you two letters dated 5 and 7 September which took exactly one month to get here. In your letters you write that most important now is that I find a way to get to Kishinev or Warsaw although I don't see how. It would take a lot of money and permissions for the family all together to get that far but perhaps you are thinking that I go first, then return to get them. This is a difficult and risky step but nonetheless to avoid further suffering I am getting ready for the trip.*
>
> *Within days I will leave for a certain village where I will be able to get more information about this journey because no one knows about these things in Nikolaev. I will try to get money for this and don't foresee any problems in this matter. Most important is the crossing. I think to stop at Warsaw as that is what you seem to have in mind so prepare all necessary monies and documents in order that as soon as you receive a telegram or letter from me there will be nothing to delay you sending them on.*
>
> *We are very surprised that you haven't sent us one package. Many folks receive valuable packages now. Uncle's sister Sura who lives in Korsun and who you used to visit received from one person*

millions of rubles (70/80 dollars) so please try to send a package because they come often and many receive them. In any case without delay as soon as you get this letter prepare everything that is needed for our family and if you can Chaika [Klara] and Liuba and Veniamin and at the very least Chaika.

In two days I am going from Nikolaev to Volynsk Province from where I will write you my next letter. Most important is that you have everything ready. Perhaps it will work out well and then you'll get a letter or telegram from me from Warsaw. Be well, Isor

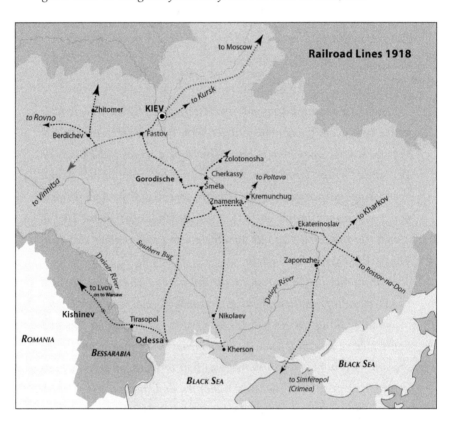

Earlier, Manya had complained to Eli about this plan that Isor go to Romania or Poland alone to get all the necessary items and money for their leaving Russia. The issue, to repeat, is that money transfers will work between the USA and Poland or Romania but won't work between Russia and the USA. Ordinary commercial relations between these two countries had yet to be established. So this plan, though risky, is somewhat reasonable. It is not reasonable to Manya, however, who writes to Eli (in Yiddish):

> Today you write that Aser [Isor] should travel to Rumania or Poland. How can he travel? We need money for that. And how can he do such a thing successfully? You should realize that he is now my taylne [part of me]. He reads my thoughts. He makes up for the unfortunate situation of our son, Meer [whom we have lost].

No doubt, Manya would feel a great insecurity without the steadying hand of her oldest son. Yet the mood of Manya and her family must brighten after she gets a letter from Eli that he has sent two packages with food. The letter was written in the fall of 1921, October or November, but the exact month is undecipherable due to poor handwriting. This is now the second letter *from* Eli that is available. Eli as before writes in Yiddish. *Dear Mali and my dear little children. Today I just returned from New York. I paid 20 dollars and you will receive two packages with food. I am still not able to send money. I think Chaika should travel as well. Please Mali, write precisely about our son Meer. How many tears I have already shed. I have written separately to Oser [Isor]. I send regards to Rivele, Yosele, Nechmale.*

Mali is the diminutive for Manya. *Rivele, Yosele, Nechmale* are Yiddish diminutive names for Eli's children (Rivka, Iosif, and Niuma). Ida (sometimes Ita), now 15, seems to have been forgotten in the above passage. Notice that Eli is remembering his children as dear "little" children. Eight years have passed. Iosif, the second youngest has already become *Bar Mitzvah*. All the children are in their teens except Niuma, who is eleven and Isor, now the head of the family, at 21 years old.

Eli's expectations of early success exceed reality. He writes to Manya in Yiddish on December 11, 1921 that he is *sure* the family has received the packages he has sent. *Little packages of shoes and undergarments. And a big package with more shoes for everyone and dresses and outfits for the children and other things.*

He adds: *I await a telegram from Isor. As soon as I receive that I can send money.* To repeat, Eli is working with the conception that Isor will be traveling to Kishinev or Warsaw where he can receive money. *When I receive a telegram from you it will become a little easier for you. I will immediately send money and you will travel to me. I will wait another week or two. If I don't have a letter from you or a telegram I will immediately send you passage for the ship (ship cards/billets) and money and when you receive the ship billets with the money prepare immediately for departure. Do not schlep any baggage on board. Bed linens if you have any. If you don't, don't worry. When you arrive with the children everything will be here for you. Write to Chaika to also come to you and I will also send her a ship billet. . . . I think you will need to travel via Kovno (Lithuania). But when I send you all the ship billets I will give you full instructions. Perhaps you will need to travel another route. I will send to Chaika all the papers she needs.*

January 9, 1922

> *Dear Papa,*
>
> *Your letter dated December 4 we received. Of your packages we have received not even one. We await them each day. We have received all your instructions. No doubt you are aware that I did cross the border but for various reasons I had to return back here.*
>
> *We have decided that as soon as we receive all your packages we will leave Russia. But because we have received nothing, we can't even think about it. All is ok with us but living is unbearable. Inflation is awful and there is hunger. A funt of bread costs 25 rubles. There is no work. All the same we try one way or another to make it through but it's horribly difficult.*
>
> *Correspond with Uncle Meir and write your letters more clearly more detailed. You, for instance, in one and the same letter write that you are sending us . . . what? and that you are going . . .where? To Nikolaev for us with packages or ?? Rumors are floating that there is a ship from New York in Odessa but we don't know exactly. As soon as we receive the packages we will start on our journey. That's what I think. It will be necessary to wait and to suffer still, we'll see how circumstances develop. Your son, Isor*

These rumors about a "ship from New York in Odessa" had everything to do with the beginning of humanitarian food aid from

America. The American Relief Administration was now helping to relieve starvation in Southern Ukraine by sending food supply ships to the Port of Odessa. But as far as Manya's family is concerned, their future depends on the packages, sent months ago in the fall of 1921.

Jan 11,1922

Nikolaev

Dear Papa,

I am alive and well. And hope you are too. I am waiting for our departure for America. It is difficult to live here for us. Try to get us to you. Riva

Dear Papa,

We are awaiting your packages which you sent to us. We wait with impatience. Ita

Dear Papa,

I am alive and well and wish the same for you. We sent the health certificates to you. I kiss you. Iosif

Dear Papa,

I am alive and well. I have nothing more to write. Beniamin

Another long month goes by.

February 20, 1922

Dear Papa,

We received your letter of December 28, 1921 but we have received no packages. Without packages we cannot begin our journey to you. Riva

Dear Papa,

I am alive and well. We received your letter of December 25 [sic]. We think by Passover we will be with you. Your son, Iosif

Most beloved friend Eli,

I still have not received any bundles of food. I wait every day for them to come. God should only help me and I should hear from our child [Meer]. I wrote to Chaika that she should come. Mali

Again, Eli's expectations exceed reality. He writes on February 25, 1922 in Yiddish.

To My Dear Beloved Wife Molly and to my dear little children,

I pray to God that I will hear that you have all departed — and that you have already received the ship cards (tickets) with the money and the packages. I would write you more but I think that by the time my letter arrives you will already be on the road. Please, if you write, please write the address correctly with the house number and the name of the street. . . If you yet receive my letter, if it's possible for you when you arrive in Kovno (Lithuania), do telegraph me.

I send regards to my dear son. . . that your departure be pleasant.

I send regards to my daughter Revele, when you arrive you will not be so angry at me.

I send regards to my daughter Yutele [Ida]. Why don't you write me any regards?

I send regards to my son Yosele and my son Niumele. I kiss you all from the bottom of my heart. From me your father who hopes to be together with all of you.

Eli's eagerness is endearing, And now it seems the packages are on their way to Eli's niece Celia Rubenstein in Moscow. Writing to Eli in December 1921, she says she is waiting for the packages destined for Manya.

December 25, 1921
Moscow
Dear Uncle,

I was happy to receive from you . . . two letters. I haven't answered waiting for the package to arrive but so far nothing has come. Don't worry Uncle as soon as I get the package I will send it on to them. I am well aware of their situation and also await with impatience the package as it will be good to get it and send it on and give them something to feel happy about. . . .

. . . It's hard to live in the 20th Century. . . . They (our family) has suffered much unhappiness. I don't know much about them. I did get a letter from a friend in Odessa with their address. I'll write them now, in case I get something back. From Yasha I have nothing. From Beti I have two letters. My poor sister. She wants to help everyone but she has no means to do so. Oh how do they live? I ache for her. I'll write her today too. Be well, write more often.

My husband and daughter greet you,

Your niece

At this time when Manya's family are feeling more and more hopeful they will be able to leave, her brother Veniamin in Kiev writes to Eli in a most despairing fashion. In a letter dated February 10, 1922, he first thanks his brother-in-law for the notification from the All Russian Jewish Public Committee for Relief of Pogrom and War Sufferers that a package will come for him from Eli. Then he states how nearly impossible it now seems for the hopes that he, his wife Liuba and "at least Chaika" could travel with Manya and family. Indeed he has become very discouraged and despairing, even if somewhat misinformed. (Chaika is Klara's Yiddish name.)

Dear Eli,

My heart aches for the pains that you and your family are enduring. How much vitality, money and energy you waste in order to get Mali to you. All this is useless . . . getting to America is impossible because America lets no one in aside from woman and children up to the age of 18. You think your preparations are sufficient for Mali and the children and even Chaika to depart. One needs first to get to Kovno (Lithuania) and even if that is successful, what would be the use if America isn't letting anyone in. Many people who get to Poland are stuck because they can't go to America regardless. . . . I fear that all that you do will not have the hoped for result. My advice: Get Mali and the children registered to travel lawfully and then we will be able to give thought to the rest of us. Get your instructions from the American Bureau of the Jewish Social Committee that helps the victims of pogroms, 47 West 42nd Street, NYC. I know this because I was working at this Jewish Committee until today.

Veniamin (sometimes spelled as Beniamin) is misinformed regarding the chances of success of the plan now being worked out by Isor, but he is right about the dwindling chances of any other member of Eli's family (other than his wife and children) being able to emigrate to America. Chaika, as we will see, did not have the correct papers to leave with Manya and her family. (Isor leaves her ticket at the Baltic-American Shipping Lines office in Riga.) The USA was indeed beginning to clamp down on immigration with the Emergency Immigration Act of 1921 culminating in the final curtain: the Immigration Act of 1924. In fact all of Manya's siblings—whether willingly (Mokha) or unwillingly (Chaika, Veniamin, and his wife Liuba)—stayed in Russia.

Liuba appends Veniamin's letter with a gracious few sentences disguising her disappointment. *I would be overjoyed if we could travel to America. But we can't think about it until you get your family out and then you'll be able to think about us. Meanwhile your package will be very useful for us and I thank you very much for not forgetting about us.*

Finally, after months of waiting and no doubt suffering, for the Great Famine was in full display as the reports from Raskin to the American Relief Association's bosses show, the packages arrive.

March 29, 1922—Moscow

Dear Uncle!

Three days ago I received a package for Aunt Manya. Included were: five pairs of warm underwear, one pair of boots, three pairs of stockings . . . I get letters frequently from Manya she is waiting

164

for this with impatience. In the Ukraine there is famine. People are dying like flies.

You know Uncle that you could help and support them even more significantly than with these packages. Because the items you sent are for cold weather and they aren't needed now, spring is here and to sell them won't bring too much money. The season has passed. Much better and much quicker would be a food package through the American Committee for Aid. This is a very useful package and you can send even several. A package costs 10 dollars and it arrives within six (?) weeks to Moscow. Three poods [1 pood=36 pounds] of food stuffs. That translates into 50 million rubles worth of stuff. We can get these but only for now in Moscow.

March 30

I interrupted this letter because I got notice that the second package has arrived and today I went and got it. I am so glad that we have both packages now. It has been so long and this is the first signs of help for Aunt Manya. Now for some reason, it was necessary to pay customs fee, I paid 3.5 million rubles. That's of course not easy but the important thing is we have it now: 3 pair of women's boots, 1 pair of men's boots, 3 pair of stockings . . . I already telegraphed Aunt Manya; no doubt someone will come for this. Meanwhile I will try to get a package of foodstuffs from the American Committee for Aid in advance on your account, then it won't be so hard for them.

I wish you a good Passover.

Your niece,

Celia Rubenstein

Note the extraordinary inflation since 1917. Folks using ruble figures in the *millions*. Example: the customs fees of 3.5 million. The fact that one package of goods from the USA can be resold for tens of millions of rubles. Note also that the packages arrive on the very day before Passover. Passover in 1922 was March 31. Iosif's hope they would be in America before Passover doesn't happen, but knowing the packages have arrived (because Celia would telegraph them this news that day) was almost as good. Although what this eighth Passover looked like in the land of Nikolaev where food was practically non-existent, we don't know.

The packages take another long month to arrive from Moscow to Nikolaev. They arrive on April 29, 1922. We have the affidavit to that effect. After that we have no information from Manya or Isor until they have left the Soviet Union and are in another country, Latvia. In the city of Riga. Certainly the excitement must be great. The only sorrow from Manya is that she knows she is leaving a dead son, Meer, somewhere in the miasma of Russia, having never heard anything from the Russian Army. She knows she must give up all hope.

Manya signs April 21, 1922 package receipt.

Riga, September 13

To my beloved father!

Yesterday we arrived at last in Riga. In other words, we left Russia and we are already in a new land that is called Latvia, at the office of the Baltic American Line where we have finished the necessary formalities. Today we are going to the American consulate to get our visas to travel to America. What is not very pleasant is only our cobbled together circumstances as we have to wait two weeks because the ship leaves the 26th September. We will travel on a ship called the "Lithuania." This letter will certainly arrive before we arrive in New York.

Telephone, Bryant 2016   Cable Address "EVKOM" New York

THE ALL RUSSIAN
JEWISH PUBLIC COMMITTEE
For Relief of Pogrom and War Sufferers
110 WEST 40TH STREET
NEW YORK CITY

BUREAU OF THE REPRESENTATIVE
IN THE UNITED STATES AND CANADA

July 8, 1922.

Eli Brodansky
818 W. 2nd St
Wilmington, Del.

Dear Sir:

Re: Application # 24001

We wish to inform you that we have received a signed receipt for delivery in Russia of
your parcel #24001____. The receipt is enclosed
herein.

Kindly acknowledge receipt of this
letter together with the enclosure.

Yours very truly,

AMERICAN BUREAU OF THE
ALL RUSSIAN JEWISH PUBLIC COM.

Per_____

Package receipt letter to Eli.

Today the office gave us a copy of the telegram that has now been
sent to you, saying that we have arrived in Riga and you should
send us our money: $200. Actually, we used almost all our money to
pay for the ship's tickets, second class. Almost all of the immigrants
travel second class because, we are told, the ocean is not very calm
now and above all, it is extremely unpleasant in the lowest hold of
the ship for the passengers in third class. You might say that's a lot
of money to pay for second class and to use up most of our resources

this way but only we are so exhausted from the journey, that we want to travel a little more comfortably. Chaika is not traveling with us because her papers were not ready. Her ticket remains meanwhile in the ship's office. We all look very good, and are dressed very well and are waiting with great patience for the time when we will be together.

All the best from your son Isor.

Manya adds:

Much beloved Friend Eli,

Know that we find ourselves, thank God, in good health and that we are in Riga now. We had, thank God, a good trip here. Many people are traveling. We have good company; Bayle the American travels with us, together with Mendl Zayde's niece. . . .But the only thing, God should help me, I am traveling away from my child. Dear friend, you can understand how great the pain is for me that I am traveling away from Meer. I hear absolutely nothing. God knows where his bones are already. . . . Be healthy my friend, and God should help us that we should come to you in peace, and we beg God for a good new year. I really wish that Chaika was also traveling together with us and even though I still hope she will be with us, it is still very good. Stay healthy.

From me, your friend, that will soon be with you,
Mali

For all the excitement of finally being on their way—and despite the fact I have my father's cheery diary written beginning the day they left Kiev and detailing the ship's oceanic crossing to their arrival in America—the enormity of this *finale* shows up in an essay my father wrote seven years after he was in America, at the age of 19. He titled this essay "Nights on a Boat."

NIGHTS ON A BOAT

A ship on the ocean. The longed-for ocean. The promised land.

I did not yet know America. I was trying to forget bloody Europe. On the ocean I was free. The days were warm and gay. But the nights reshaped scenes from the past. There stride across my vision burly peasants with axes, clubs, stones, grunts, chasing a child: it runs, stumbles, falls; the peasants throw themselves upon its little body, pound upon the little life, and when they have done their beastly work, there is left only blood and bones. "Take them away from here, all of them, into the fields, drive them, rout them!" A company of Cossacks eyes a bunch of wailing women and children. A rush of horses, and little heads and soft bodies are crushed under the iron legs of the horses. The screaming and wailing is over, only moans of the dying.

I cannot come to wakefulness. There come again before me pictures indistinct, edgeless. Hungry children wandering aimlessly on hot city streets. Their eyes, falling on bricks or stones, plead, Why is it not bread? Why so many hard bricks, why so little bread? Here and there lying in gutters, a body with a bloated stomach, a leg already mutilated by dogs. Black heavy flies swarm around new meat.

A hand wakes me up. And now, once conscious, I know in front of me is America. Where nobody is afraid. And I am going there! And nobody will stop me! Yet the dreaded thought: the captain might lose course and bring us back from where we came. How I prayed that nothing would happen to the boat.

* * * * *

My mother and my father—from whence they came—couldn't have been more opposite. My mother, born in Nebraska, of activist, passionate idealists dedicated to making a better world imbibed these dreams and ideals of her parents. To the extent life allowed her, she took on the socialist ideals and beliefs of both her parents. Her habits were those of study, reading, and study. I knew the contents of the storage bin she left when she died. So many files with so many notes about so many important subjects: global peace, social justice, United Nations, workers' rights, women's rights, humanitarianism, Unitarianism, historical/political reviews of global conflicts and efforts at resolution. My mother was free in this way, free to dream *and believe*. She never experienced the pain and agony of living in Russia.

My father, on the other hand, had come to America *with* the experience of the pain and agony of living in Russia. His young life witnessed much cruelty and despair: without a father during war, revolution, and more war, he had to have inhaled a helplessness his mother Manya faced as waves of political, economic and social chaos—as well as the unleashed ugliness of the peasant's fist—finally overwhelmed them. For my father, I believe, American gave him the chance to leave that behind *forever*. To turn away from history and its underbelly. To delight in his earthly and artistic talents and powers.

They could not understand each other, my mother and my father. Yes, they were scythe against stone.

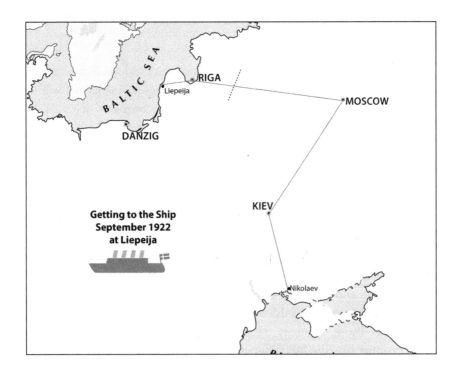

24. Olga

I never did hanky panky with any of the American men I worked with during my trips to Russia. My reputation was pristine and easily kept because I didn't drink, not after that first picnic during my first visit to the Russian Far East.

I love to swim in oceans warm and blue and was certainly wanting to be cooperative. We sat on the ground in a circle. Our hosts supplied us with breads and cold cuts, endlessly delivering toasts—short and sweet, long and foolish. That meant lots of vodka. Even though that day I only sipped, because someone is filling up your glass at every instance, in enough time I was flat out drunk. I lay in my bed that night refusing all the insistent phone calls to, please, I should come to Room So-and-So for more partying. I was much too dizzy, my head swirling. The next day—the day for my presentation in front of the entire assembly—I was still dizzy and aswirl. Olga, sitting close and directly in front of me had to whisper encouragement even as I had a written copy from which I was reading my Russian speech. The hangover, I decided, had despoiled my work, the reason why I had been invited and the purpose for which I was there. I would lose respect if that continued. So from that day on, I might put my lips to the glass of vodka but neither sip nor swallow. Just like the guy who said he puffed but did not inhale. The afternoon after my participation in the conference session ended, Olga, cat-like and sexy as she was—after all, these *Intourist* guides (KGB agents) were meant to beguile men, not women scholars—asked me to go along with her back to the beach. She had lost the top to her bathing suit the night before.

Olga was my interpreter, guide, and security agent on that first trip and for many trips thereafter. Over the years we became friends. I visited her mother in Moscow when her mother was dying, bringing with me various packets of flower seeds for her window box. She was, it seemed, very, very sick.

Even after I stopped traveling, and had sold my publishing business, Olga and I visited in the U.S., spending a week together. She and her academic professorial husband were living in Japan at the time. He was on a lecture tour in the U.S., one of their stops was Seattle.

Olga and I took a trip together spending three days and nights on Fiddlehead Farm, a working farm near Powell River, north of Vancouver's Sunshine Coast. On that trip Olga tried to tell me everything she could about everything I asked. I believe she was sincere.

In answer to one of my questions, Olga tried to explain why in the Stalinist era, brothers reported on sisters, children on their parents, parents on their parents, aunts and uncles. She tried to explain to me how a person can become so mentally deranged. Sometimes she talked just too fast or too emotively and I couldn't comprehend. I wouldn't tell her, however, for that would stop the spell.

It was our second night at Fiddlehead Farm and we were heading to the sauna, a dry sauna. The moon was full with a red ring around it. Olga was very superstitious. "That's a bad moon," she had said. There was always something going on with the moon for Olga and always something going on about atmospheric pressures. She was telling me, it seemed, about her father's father, a Jew. But I could not catch everything. Of course I thought later, the whole territory I was reporting on, learning about, doing business with, was peopled by either exiles (Jews and non-Jews), Cossacks (sent to defend the territory), or "pioneers" enticed to settle there by promises of land grants and prosperity. Except for the barely visible indigenous peoples, everyone was either a child, or grandchild of exiles, prisoners, pioneers, Cossacks, or newly arrived. Olga's mother's family were "pioneers" from the Baltics. Olga's father's father had been a prisoner. A Jew.

I couldn't understand everything she was telling me. I had to let it go by. There wasn't any other way. You know it's damn important, you don't get the gist, yet you can't stop someone and say I am not understanding, start all over again, start slowly, not when they are entrusting you with something very real and very deep and very *emotional*. Many of our conversations were a mix: sometimes in Russian, sometimes in English. I preferred that Olga speak Russian because I know we always express our thoughts better in our original language. Communicating in different languages requires great skill — the art of translation, the art of interpretation. I have read that sixty percent of content gets lost in translation. Sixty percent!

Ah, Olga! She had to have slept with her various bosses; otherwise how could she have been in the relatively privileged position she was in. Yes, she was a talented *Intourist* guide and envied by her confrères for she could keep foreigners engaged much longer than they. That was a good thing. The goal was always to get to know who your foreigners are and what they are up to. Yes, Olga could be depended on for her strong work ethic.

My relationship with Olga spanned twenty years. I knew her first husband who also was in the security forces. Perhaps this sleeping-with-bosses business was before she married. They had one child who, when I last saw Olga, was studying in Australia. Olga. . . where is she now?

It was on the train ride to Vladivostok in 1988, as the first American scholar to be officially received in the then still closed city, when she showed me how it is done: this seduction business. We were in a very crowded railroad bar car where everyone was drinking and smoking. Olga too. Like a little kid never having seen this before I watched as she took her glass of whatever and drank keeping her eyes the whole time on some one other person far beyond those around her in that crowded car. We were cabin mates, she and I. I told her I was going to retire early. She said, she'd be along soon. I didn't see her until the next morning. Perhaps those eyes were on her then-to-become Police Chief husband? I have never seduced anyone Olga-style. I have never allowed myself/permitted myself/felt powerful in myself to ever even try.

No Russian ever made an advance to me. It was simply out of bounds. All Russian behavior toward me, in my opinion, was scripted or prescribed, prescribed, or circumscribed and anything and everything was certainly reported by Soviet/Russian agents tasked with this. This was regardless or whether or not I was suspicious. It was just their *de facto* way of dealing.

Even when they were drunk, Russians knew their limits. Yes they can get very, very drunk, and when a young punk American takes the challenge then he, the both of them, can get crawling-on-the-floor drunk. I hated that stuff. Loathed it in fact. And only once witnessed such things. I had arranged to bring a small group of us to Vladivostok to teach employees of a large fishing company the elements of market economics. (Russian policy at that time supporting these efforts.) After a day's work, we were invited to enjoy dinner on a mid-summer night sail. During the outing, a diver descended into the waters to catch all sorts of marvelous ocean fish, shellfish, eel, etc. These ingredients for the ship's chef to make the most wonderful soup of the sea I have ever tasted. Soup to go along with the vodka. And vodka enough for a drinking contest if there were any takers. A young American on our team at that time, a computer specialist, 23 years old, took the challenge from an older Russian man. And so I watched while they did their thing until yes, truly, while trying to climb a set of stairs that led from where we were below to the upper deck from where we needed to disembark neither of them could. Both would fall back to the floor until they were helped.

No, Russian men I didn't have to worry about. They were constrained, watched, edited. American men were completely different. They were in the opposite situation from the Russians. Unobserved by their home society, loosened from all mores, from all wives, from all witnesses, and actually *encouraged* to party with Russian women; women who were always young, always beautiful, lithe, slender, demure and refined. Russian women easily deflected any particular attention to me that might have been made by an American man. I never felt that kind of attention on me but once. Again, the vodka. We were celebrating a signing of a cooperative agreement (makes the purpose of the trip seem worthwhile and getting things in writing with the approval of governors does help next steps) so can't say the celebration was celebrating something vapid, but the drinking was always probably more to the purpose from the point of view of the Russian men than to forecast and celebrate any *real* possibilities for business together. I was caught unawares when the American CEO of one of the companies participating in the delegation, the delegation's leader, placed a big sloppy kiss on my half-open mouth.

I wonder if anyone else took note. I got pretty rigid as time went on. As soon as I could gracefully excuse myself, I'd go back to my hotel room for a good night's sleep. I needed that. It was obligatory really for me. Let them carouse, let them bring in the Russian girls or go to the steam baths then find the Russian women. I'd go back to my hotel room to prepare for the next day.

* * * * *

"Mom! Who 's that?" My daughter in her mid-twenties was on the phone.

It was past midnight and she had caught me without an excuse. He had answered the telephone in our Seoul Hotel in the middle of the night for I never thought it would be my daughter and I otherwise spoke no Korean. "My friend and I are still up, Ladybug, planning for tomorrow's conference." I was lying. She knew it. I knew she would know it. And so from that day on, I have admitted to my daughter and to whomever else happens to be listening, that yes I had had a Korean boyfriend. And that was happening during the last year I was married. Yes I had had an affair. Yes, my daughter caught me. But except for the three-word phrase—"my Korean boyfriend"—we have never spoken more about it.

There have been times of considerable land distances between my daughter and myself and, more to the point, considerable emotional distances: chasms and divides, caused by great earthquakes, by the rubbing of tectonic plates; Grand Canyon type distances between us where a call from one ridge top to another never reaches but falls into eerie silence far below; barren landscapes from volcanic eruptions the sizes of those of Mount Vesuvius or Mount Hood. Yet at other times my daughter and I seem to be almost one. These then are the moments where the terrain we are on is a flowering high mountain meadow we've reached together, places where only benevolent nature presides, places where the sun warms our hearts and Mom can watch her daughter frolic and revel in ice-cold but wonderful mountain lakes, places where the feeling abounds that there is nothing to worry about, we are one.

My daughter knows me. I think she accepts me. I accept her but I do not know if she knows that. Maybe she doesn't know me, but she tracks me. I accept her even though I do not, cannot, track her.

What does she mean to me? My daughter? Continuity. I will say goodbye to her when I am dying and she will say goodbye to me and it will be very, very meaningful. That's all I know. And if we are fortunate, accompanying her will be her daughter, my granddaughter Tillie, who my whole being has loved from the first day forward, as both of them know. I feel I will be able to tell my daughter everything and she will be able to hold it. She will stay upright and know her task is to carry on. Even when we have to say goodbye. That's all I know.

We have never been like some mothers and daughters. Those who might chat easily every week or so, if not more often. Nor like those whose hostilities last years and years. We don't have heart-to-heart talks. Yet I know I am not rejected. And that somehow I even know I am accepted. Does she know now I accept her? As she is. I think she may know that now. We change. She has changed. I have changed. The quotidian part of our lives has changed as well. Yet, I feel she tracks me. I feel she is there for me. And when I write on those health forms "next of kin," or who to contact in case of emergencies, she is the right person. I hope I am, in principle, that for her.

Many times I would tell myself as I went about my motherly tasks, those tasks we call nurturing, and they are nurturing, urging her to use her gifts, her talents, study, find meaning for herself, excel in that meaning, each time I would add if I cannot manage that for myself . . . well, I must manage that for myself, so she can know. If I cannot do it, then how would she know it is possible for her to do it? Then to what purpose all that urging? And so I did both. The mother/other. Did I do it well? No. But has that doing allowed my daughter to give it her full try? Yes.

25. Al Anon

I can see it now why my son so easily took to marijuana during his freshman year of high school. It was an answer to not only his ulcerative colitis but to the emotional violence in our home. Whenever I was home, my anxiety turned ferocious, and landed on my husband. You failed! You failed *me*! You failed *us*! No wonder our son turned away from this unbearable, merciless parental conflict, and began to drop out, turn toward his music, toward marijuana, toward alcohol. He was fifteen years old.

Later, two years out of high school, our divorce final, his addiction entrenched, his best friend committed suicide. I was *not there*. I was on my way home from one of my three-week Russia trips. Flights now had layovers either in Japan or in Korea. No adult was at home. He was blaming himself.

After an exchange between him and me, he put his fist through the wall of his bedroom. After I overheard an ex-girlfriend saying she had heard he had tried something stronger than marijuana, I walked into an Al Anon meeting. Rachael had told me about this twelve-step program (for family and friends of alcoholics). Some folks there were smiling and, Yes, that program changed my life.

Amos was raised in a crucible of parental anger-violence. He took, his gut took the brunt of this. And addiction followed. I found a way in Al Anon. I learned about fear. That my forays in Russia's back country, taiga and tundra, might be seen by some as fearless but this kind of fearlessness did not exempt me from fear of the other kind. Fear for my son, fearful that he had lost any sense of well-being. This fear was different. It was driving my life, had possessed me and was harmful to us both. Al Anon taught me that the opposite of fear is not fearlessness but faith. Faith? That had no familiar ring to it for me, no resonance anywhere prior. Faith was something unfamiliar to me, something that my mother had rejected. No matter the faith (or was it, adherence to religious customs) of my father. OK, I say, granted I was siding (incoherently to be sure) with my mother during the throes of her struggles against my father. After all, she was *against* my father. For it was she who installed a lock with a bolt on their bedroom door, wanting to keep him out. A very conspicuous lock for a simple door in our 100-year old Connecticut farmhouse where we lived. Troubled and upset witnessing her pain, I determined I would have nothing but disregard for any wishes or pressures coming from my father. No willingness to explore faith, much less Jewish faith. Yet, years later, I went along with Al Anon's twelve-step program because I was suffering from the consequences of my son's addiction: that slippery slope where loss begets loss; losing begets losing, and the family isolates.

In Al Anon, I found a calm that has been vital to my life ever since, that the God of my understanding is the God I sit with when I create, is the God with whom I have a contract to create, is that loving space I find when I seek it, is the Universe where I am supported in ways that I could never have anticipated when I put my trust there. The phrase from *Proverbs* to "trust the universe (God) with all your might and lean not into your understanding" is the best piece of learning I've still to better. And that is what I can say is my faith.

With help from my daughter, the support of Amos' father, and the services of a talented (and Jewish) interventionist, seven us got together. Here we were: myself and Chuck, my mother (Amos' beloved Grandma), my sister (his beloved aunt Molly), his sister Rachael, her friend Aimee (like a cousin to Amos), and the only one of his friends willing to participate in this uncertain event, Cameron. Cameron was a sober, serious kind of guy. Amos had known him since they were both babies. They had stayed in contact. It was Cameron who Amos agreed to drive with to the airport where a seaplane was scheduled to fly to Nanaimo on Vancouver Island, B.C. just North of Seattle where staff from Edgewood, an established and well-respected treatment center, were waiting for him.

Although my son's life a decade after treatment had been ups and downs, not one ounce of life, spirit, purpose has been snuffed out. And years afterwards, Amos was nominated for Seattle's Art-Innovator of-the-Year award. *For the work he does with kids making music.* He also led a group of his students to the Obama White House invited for a week-long program, Music of the Civil Rights Era, an honor *for the work he does with kids making music.* And more nominations: for Seattle's coveted Artist-of-the Year award *for the work he does with kids making music.* Then the nomination for a Grammy *for the song he produced with kids.*

Amos was raised in a crucible of unbearable parental conflict. Yet, the crucible has made this man, of whom I am unceasingly proud.

Yes, my daughter had introduced me to Al Anon. Ten years later, my son introduced me to Vipassana Meditation. We might compare these meditation practices to some within the Jewish tradition. I don't. Vipassana meditation has provided me another tool for peaceful daily work. It is for this that my son and I have been able to sit together and talk in a most meaningful way of his experience as a child, who being very, very sick needed his mother so badly and who couldn't reach her because she was, for 55 long days, for all practical purposes, nowhere.

So the generations march on. The Jewish passion, ideals and activism of my mother's parents; the Jewish suffering, horrendous historical events of my father's family. Then a union of these two children of very different backgrounds: my mother with her passion to continue the idealism and the activism of her revolutionary parents, my father with his passion to leave his story behind and to create, celebrate, enjoy new-found freedoms. These two create a union, beget children despite the near-impossible feat to find common ground between them. Yes, they beget three children. I am their middle child and how badly I want, I try, to unmake that palpable disunion, which somehow had wormed its way into me.

26. A Plot in the Jewish Section

I know now that tefillin are not "ornaments." They are a physical representation of a commitment. It is action: to wear the tefillin, to put on the tefillin, to say the accompanying prayers. Not ornaments, not even like a Jewish star you wear on your necklace as a marker of identity.

How can it be that I actually gave my granddaughter a Jewish star for her necklace? Something I never ever would have done before, yet now I have. For me, her Jewish ornament becomes—always and all too quickly—the infamous star sewn on to outer wear, that then becomes Jewish stars inside holding pens, fenced areas, and then the trains or the fields . . . My granddaughter Tillie wears her necklace with pride, but my unquenchable fear knows others see with other associations.

It is all about differing associations, isn't it? Like whenever I am in the steam room after a morning swim at our athletic club and the steam comes on, so does the gas spigot where we are huddled, naked and soon to be asphyxiated.

After my second divorce, I lived with that friend of mine who had built a logging camp on the very same grounds as a former gulag camp. And who, besides being a swashbuckler and a Gentile, was nonetheless a brilliant and thoughtful partner. We often traveled together. One trip was to Amsterdam. I chose to visit the Jewish Museum there. (He chose Antique Cars.) I chose to look at the photos of the chain-link fence constructed by the occupying Nazis in the very middle of the city, in the very middle of the town square. The photo shows adults and children with our six-pointed stars on their outer clothing inside the fence while folks on the outside are walking past with the air of ordinary folks on ordinary missions on an ordinary day.

Ordinary folks *inside* fences, ordinary folks *outside* fences: indelibly etched in my being. When he and I returned from that trip, it was gardening season and he wanted to build a chain-link fence because we live where deer roam. The deer eat everything from raspberries to roses, rabbits devour all lettuce, and raccoons threaten whole rows of corn. I understood—fences keep our garden produce protected—yet

I could not, I repeat, I could not countenance a chain-link fence in my own yard. Nevermind the entirely different purpose. My partner did not understand.

Wearing the tefillin is an action which a person undertakes to show that we are a people willing to seek, discern, find, and commune with that which is divine.

And those who wear the tefillin every day do so because that practice is what is needed to remember. For me that would be a private thing. For others it is a community thing. I am for private prayer. I too seek to uncover . . . to commune. I cannot conceive ever of wearing the tefillin (although I never got the chance to try) but I can conceive of setting time aside for contemplation. Yet Michal, my friend from Israel, says that's not good enough. Prayer is communal. That's what *minyan* is all about, she tells me. "Take the Covenant," our Rabbi offered. "God is asking you to act, then you will come to understand."

Sometime after my father died, the puny accumulated knowledge of Jewish life became not enough. Yes I could answer some questions. How, for instance, did I distinguish my Jewish faith from the Christian: We talk directly to God. We do not feel we were born as sinners, so we do not think much about a hell or a heaven afterlife. Our job is to do what is right, now. Right now, with what is in front of me. The beautiful *Yom Kippur* directive: to acknowledge our travesties and then make our amends directly to the person to whom we ask forgiveness when possible. But that just about covered the whole *shebang*. Yet something was compelling me toward knowing more. And when the opportunities arose to visit Jewish museums, I jumped: Amsterdam, Berlin, Paris, Basil. I wanted to learn in these museums. *I am learning about my people. I am learning about me. I am comfortable here, learning about my people, learning about me. I am welcomed here, accepted here — automatically. I do not feel strain. I do not feel separate.* Even if I have never kissed a Jewish boy.

* * * * *

Recently I went to visit my brother in Connecticut who lives near Temple Beth Shalom (now Temple Beth Shalom *Rodfe Zedek*). The temple where my brother became Bar Mitzvah, where my father was president for many years, where I would join him on an occasional Friday night for services.

On the last day of my visit, I wanted to visit the nearby cemetery in Deep River where both our father and our mother have gravestones. My brother obliged me. I am very excited because I have learned they have started the ground work needed for an expansion and the new area is adjacent to where my mom's gravestone is, just on the boundary line. I am third on the list for new plots. Maybe I will have a space next to my mother. I am *crazy*. I wanted Mom to be in the same cemetery as Dad, even though they were divorced for over 40 years. Even though he has a shared headstone with Mary his wife of thirty years. Even though he put a Jewish star on her casket. Still, my brother and my sister obliged me. And so that's why Mom is there too.

What am I doing? Trying to put us all back together again—that's exactly what I am doing. The Temple office was open. I wanted to confirm I am still third on the list for new plots. In this new building I notice a plaque with my father's name as a former president. As a daughter of his I am accorded, at least so it seems, a plot as I have requested. I want my headstone to read: Elisa Brodinsky, mother of Rachael and Amos, grandmother of Tillie Hope and Liev Aditieh.

I understand now, and I claim my place in the chain of Jewish tradition.

AFTERWORD

My knowledge of Russian defined my career, and much of my adult life. At 21, I began learning the language, and made a career using that tool. Russian is a mother tongue of my father (along with Yiddish). He and I together deciphered and translated the one single handwritten letter he showed me from his mother Manya, the one he put on the dining room table during one of my visits. The several hundred others that Manya and her children wrote to Eli in America formed the basis of this chronicle. They told the story my father did not, would not.

My father and I spoke only once about pogroms. He told me about Cousin Shimeon's tongue. But I knew about this ancient form of punishment from the movie, *Andrei Rublev*, about the famous icon painter who lived in the 14th century. An early scene in the movie shows a Jew jesting in a barn for an audience of peasants. His commentary is brilliant biting and truthful. The authorities come, knock him out, haul him away. Later in another scene, he is back to jesting with half of a tongue, half a speech.

Only silence. The ghosts of the tundra, the silence of the Russian taiga helped me know who I am.

I was not there at my father's death. I was in Seattle. He was in Connecticut. Only my brother's wife was there. He died agitated, she told us, crying out *Ma, Ma*.

I don't know how much my father shared with his father about those eight years of his young life in Russia while the family waited to get to America to join him. I only know what he didn't share with me.

I am preparing for my 75th Passover as I write. It will be at my home but my daughter's husband will lead the seder service as he did last year. Her daughter Tillie and I will clean out the wax from the candleholders and polish Elijah's and Miriam's cups. My son will come. His son Aditieh and I will make the place cards copying names from a list of the guests we have invited—both Jews and Gentiles. My daughter will coordinate a fabulous meal. My son will play the piano to our songs.

Maybe my contribution to our people is to give what cousin Shimeon could not give, and what my father would not tell. Their story, their tongue. My story; my tongue. *Dayenu. It is enough.*

THE END

ACKNOWLEDGMENTS

I thank my reader-enthusiasts: Soula Stephanopoulos, Karen Wilken, Emily Orrson, Keith Winzenreid, Molly Boggis, Alan Kahn, Nitza Rosovsky.

I give thanks to Rabbis Norman Hirsch and Elana Zaiman for leading me to Rabbi Beth Lieberman; to literary agents Janet Rosen and Sherry Bykovsky for their support along the path to publication, and to Alessandra Anzani and Kira Nemirovsky at Academic Studies Press for shepherding the manuscript into print. I owe gratitude to Adam Langer, Culture Editor at the *Forward*; my essay "Moscow on the Delaware" (April 8, 2015) was the precursor of this book.

I am indebted to Gail Harker, Marilyn Milberger, Susan Prescott, and especially to Roosje Wiedijk and Joe Menth for graphic and cartographic expertise. I give thanks to Karen Wilken and Sarah Rose Olsen for editorial assistance.

Thank you to Caraid O'Brien, Miriam Koral, Michal Jacoby, Sam Roskin, Alexandra Kaufman, and Alexander Belyaev for providing invaluable translation help.

I give special thanks to my editor, Rabbi Beth Lieberman, for unfailing accompaniment on this journey. And finally, I give thanks to Tillie Hope Kahn who was ready to design the cover on the first day I told her I was writing a book.

ABOUT THE AUTHOR

Elisa Brodinsky Miller's contributions to academic and journalistic literature on the subject of Soviet/Russian Far East commercial relations with Asia and the USA have spanned forty years. Writing from the University of Washington's School of Business and the Jackson School of International Studies between 1975 and 1995, her articles can be seen in many publications including *Soviet Geography, Columbia Journal of World Business, Trends in Organized Crime,* and *Far Eastern Economic Review.* She has contributed chapters in multiple books: *Rubles and Dollars: Strategies for Doing Business in the Soviet Union; The Russian Far East and Pacific Asia; Soviet American Horizons on the Pacific.*

Dr. Miller's unique research grant to the Soviet Far East in 1988 allowed the field work that subsequently would aid many American clients who had a newfound interest in trans-Pacific, Russian-American relations. Of her many consulting activities, she aided the State of Alaska's pioneering efforts to melt the "ice curtain" and ultimately became Soviet/ Russian advisor to Alaska Airlines which resulted in a US-USSR bilateral flight agreement in 1989. As the Director of the North Pacific Round Table, Miller played a prominent role in Seattle's 1990 Goodwill Games, organizing a delegation of governors from the Russian Far East to meet their counterparts of the Pacific Northwest.

In 1990 she founded and edited the successful newsletter *The Russian Far East Update,* published from 1990 to 1999. Alongside that endeavor her company published four editions of *The Russian Far East, A Business Reference Guide.* Her newsletter subscribers numbered 500 large and small multinational corporations and government agencies from countries around the world. She presently works in graphic narrative and lives on Whidbey Island in the State of Washington.

SOURCES

Kazaryan, P. L. *Olekminskaia Politicheskaia Ssylka: 1826–1917* [Olekminsk region as place of political exile: 1826–1917]. Yakutsk, Russia: Rossiiskaia Akademiia Nauk, 1995. Sibirskoe Otdelenie Iakutskii Institute Iazyka, Literatury i Istorii, Dalnevostochnoe Otdelenie Institut Istorii, Arkheologii i Ethnografii Narodov Dal'nego Vostoka.

Kazaryan, P. L. "Kolymskaia Politcheskaiia Ssylka, 1861–1895." In *Osvoboditel'noe Dvizhenie v Rossii I Iakutskaia Politicheskaia Ssylka* (XIX — nachalo XX v.). Yakutsk, Russia: Akademiia Nauk SSSR, 1990. Sibirskoe Otdelenie Iakutskii Institute Iazyka, Literatury i Istorii.

Kazaryan, P. L. and F. G. Safronov. *Verkhoyanskaia Politicheskaia Ssylka: 1861–1903* [Verkhoyansk region as place of political exile: 1861–1903]. Yakutsk, Russia: Iakustkoe Knizhnoe Isdatel'stvo, 1989.

APPENDIX I:

MY FATHER'S TRAVEL NOTES

Travel notes
This is the little diary my father kept during his voyage
across the ocean from his homeland in Ukraine to America.
He was twelve years old.
(My translation from the original Russian.)

GOODBYE RUSSIA

29 August 1922. We left Kiev at 12 o'clock noon.

1st of September 1922. We arrived in Moscow at night.

We spent the night in the railroad station, and at 8 am, we went into town. Because it was so early, we didn't want to wake each other up. We went to look at the nearest church, Christ the Savior.

In the garden of the church were flowers statues, vases and things.

I especially liked the clean straight streets.

3rd September. I went to a children's theatre production of DURAVA in the same building in which there was a court hearing against political antagonists. I saw different trained wild animals: swans, fox. All of them understood our language and followed instructions. For example, the rooster pulled the strings of a musical instrument with his claws. I liked most of all a dog named Ariggo Zhano Do; he could count and read our thoughts.

9th September. We left Moscow for Riga. But the train didn't go straight to Riga, but to the first station in Latvia, Zilune.

We only had tickets to the last station in the RSFSR, Sebezhe. We arrived there at 5 oclock in the afternoon. Mama gave us some Soviet coins to spend on goodies, candies, nuts.

At Sebezhe, we went through document inspection. Isor bought tickets to Zilune (Latvia). After staying at the station for one-half an hour, we were on our way toward the border. We all looked out of the windows and shouted, Goodbye Russia. Suddenly there was a booth; the train stopped. It was Soviet Inspectors. They entered, sniffed, left, and the train proceeded.

189

CROSSING THE BORDER

Having gone a few yards, we came to a stop again, we stood, stood and stood. On one side: white; on the other side: red. This meant we were at the border. A bit further there was a booth, this time it was Latvia. The train stopped, they checked documents and we then arrived at the station, Zilune.

At Zilune, we got off the train and stayed at the station for one-half hour, then got in a wagon and went to quarantine. We arrived at quarantine at night. Someone met us. We took our things. I would have rather slept, but we went a bit, then rested, then went some more. Finally we arrived.

We got to a place with straw beds. There we met one family who had crossed the border illegally. We heard a lot about crossing the border and then we went to sleep. The next morning we awoke and began the bathing process.

Women went to bathe first, they went in groups. And since everyone wanted to be first there was a lot of ruckus. Finally they were finished and it was our turn and me too. After we bathed and cleaned our area, we had to clear out. But we still had to get our belongings which had been disinfected with sulfur while we were bathing and then left for us in the sleeping rooms which had also been disinfected with sulfur.

All of our belongings were aired out, but because of the sulfur disinfectant we couldn't go into the rooms where we had slept to get them. But because it was getting time to go to the train station to catch the train to Riga, we needed to gather our belongings. We were a substantial group, about 100, but we were like one big family. We gathered around and started to discuss how we could get our things out of the sleeping rooms and decided we'd just have to go in after them, identify which belongings are yours and then run back out because it isn't possible to stay in there long or else you will suffocate. So then you have to run back in again this time, to grab them. Each held his nose with one hand and ran in. When it wasn't possible to locate one's belongings on the first try, they tried again. It was funny how each held his nose with one hand and with the other pulled out his *klumok* [bag].

Finally everything was loaded onto a push cart, some got in too, others walked behind and we reached the railroad station.

At the station we spent two hours and I feel asleep. When the train came, they woke me up and we got on. It was crowded and stuffy, but people made way for us and we settled in and fell asleep until morning. In the morning we got up. Washed up and awaited the city of RIGA.

Suddenly houses, streets appeared and we stopped. As soon as the train stopped, people came on board, street vendors and messengers. They went through the whole train offering their services. We got off the train, all around us agents: agents, agents, agents. All were shouting "Come here, come here. I can serve you better." We were looking for a hotel and didn't know what to do. We finally took an open taxi and went (we didn't know where) with one of the agents who all the time was still shouting out, offering services. Finally we stopped at a hotel named LATT.

We spent one week in RIGA and we spent it well. Mama and Isor made us bagel sandwiches everyday. Then in one big hurry in the middle of the night accompanied by rain, we left [by train]for the seaport of Libava. *[Libava is now called Liepaya.]* At Libava we arrived in the morning, it was very cold and damp. We slept a while at the train station and then we were herded out to the streets. We found a taxidriver and we went to the Russian American House.

191

AT THE SEAPORT

How much we went through in order to finally board the ship. As I already told you, we arrived in Libava in the morning, [went to Russia-America House] there our passports were collected, we were measured, and weighed and given a room with straw mattresses. We were hungry and ate lunch in a cafeteria and then we began to try to figure out when we will board the ship, when we will leave the port.

It turned out that we would have to wait a few days before we would board the ship. There was a ship (Cunard Line) which had to depart before us. During that time I learned to skate. We went to a Yiddish play.

On the 26th of September we went to a different place. We washed, a doctor inspected us, we handed over our baggage for stowage and we went to the dock and to customs. There they searched us, checking whether or not we were carrying foreign currency and then let us go on board, behind us were policemen, and we went on board in a long line.

There was our ship on which we will go to America. Music was playing. After we boarded, they took up the gangplank (walkway) and with slow movement we left the shore.

The crowd stood at the shore; some cried, some waved handkerchiefs, hats, hands. And we, we slowly pulled further from the shore all the closer to America.

ON THE SHIP

In a half hour we began to feel that which we feared would happen [seasickness]. But now was not the time to think of this, for it was time to look around! Our ship is called the "Lithuania." It is a big ship with three flags.

Having examined the ship, it was time to eat. Lunch was potatoes with herring and bread. We ate with gusto after six hours of no food. We were very hungry. We went out on deck.

We talked, made friends, and at 8 o'clock went to sleep. The deepest sleep and best dreams of my whole life.

All of us were unusually gay that this very day separates us from our former life. Now will come happiness, celebration and good living. How did we spend that first day of our 13-day trip to America? In the morning, when I awoke the ship was standing still. We were in Germany. From the ship we could see a street, a tramway, carts, cars: in a word, a city. At noon time, Isor, Riva, Ida, and Iosif went ashore. I wanted to go too, but I wasn't allowed. During this time a small ship approached ours to provision us with drinking water. I made friends with several kids and we had a lively discussion about when and how we would arrive in America. Will there be heavy seas or not.

The next day at noon we left the Port of Danzig. In two days we arrived in Copenhagen. There the ship took on passengers and finally, and only then, did we sail into open ocean. The next morning I awoke cheerful, washed but didn't want to eat. I felt languid, and understanding what this was [seasickness], went out on the deck. On deck many passengers were laying on the benches. Rather they were sitting trying to keep up their spirits, for all felt the dizziness in their heads. I couldn't walk much, and finally "the ocean took its rightful due." I laid down on the deck floor, covered by my coat, and felt better. The sailors cleaned the deck of the "mess" but otherwise did not help. You stand, you talk and suddenly you, well, throw up and are on your knees. But once I was lying down on the deck with the mist from the sea, I began to feel better. But, in a word, I lay around like this for five or six days and only two days before we arrived in New York did I begin to feel better.

Once in the evening we saw a big ship and a small ship in the distance and we began to feel a lot better, then we saw electric lights and land! Then a small, handsome looking little boat approached us, our boat stopped. But don't think we were already in America. Not so, we still had much to learn about what it means to be in America. And so our ship stopped and this handsome little all-lit-up boat approached. The small boat couldn't get close enough to us for us to let down the ladder from our boat to that one, in order to let a person climb up to our ship.

Finally, the port navigator boarded our vessel. His job is to bring the ship into port, and for this he is given 200 dollars. Foolish, honestly! There's the shore! Here we are! A turn of the wheel and that's it. I'd do it differently, I would just jump off the ship, swim to the shore because the shore is right here, in front of us. But here the navigator gets 200 dollars.

The sea (whether at this point it was sea or river, I don't know) was beautiful, waves lit up by searchlights. You could see, in the far distance, a whole row of electric street lights. We stood on the lower deck, it was dark, a slight breeze, wiping away tears. We were in America. What we had gone through to be in America.

It was late in the night but I couldn't even think of going to sleep. You would agree and say yourself, how can anyone sleep at such a time when a soul is so merry that it wants to dance, to shout. And they tell you: your job is to go to sleep!

Here comes another little ship up to us. Will our ship pass it? No, we stop, and doctors come on board our ship. Tomorrow they will examine us. But now it is time to sleep, already one o'clock in the morning.

AT ELLIS ISLAND

In the morning, we go through a long examination, and then we are taken to Ellis Island, and there we see, for the first time, the Statue of Liberty. This is a colossal representation of a woman holding a lantern in her hand. We enter a large room with many benches, surrounded by flags.

We wait almost into the evening for them to call us, there we see Negroes for the first time. They register us, ask us questions, test us (Do we know how to read?) and we then go to the "exit" room. We wanted to eat but there wasn't any place to do so.

We asked everyone what were we supposed to do, but just at that moment a man walked in and everyone was allowed to follow him. And he began to call out names, and if he calls your name (a woman told us), then they are going to let you through, but you may have to wait, even 3 to 4 days. . . . *May my stupid tongue be bitten off.**

On the second day, they called us and sat us down on a bench and we waited. Brodintsksii is how they called us. They took each of us in order and asked each of us questions. Finally it was my turn. B. Brodintsksii! And so I became became B. Brodinsky.

The family's arrival at Ellis Island was October 12, 1922, two weeks after the "Lithuania" left the Port of Liepaya (Libavo) in Latvia on September 27, 1922.

---

* *This is an old Yiddish saying. Niuma knows he will soon face the immigration authorities and perhaps he is afraid of making a mistake when answering a question.*

APPENDIX II
UNDERSTANDING THE RUSSIAN PALE

In 1914, officially, Gorodische was within the Russian Pale—a swath of territory demarcated by the Russian Imperial State within which Jews were required to live.

How did the Russian Pale come into being?

The Russian Empire in the 1600s, before Catherine the Great, was bounded on its western border by the powerful Polish-Lithuanian Commonwealth. The story of the Russian Pale begins with the story of how that territory—the Polish-Lithuanian Commonwealth formed as a union between the Kingdom of Poland and Grand Duchy of Lithuania in 1569, reaching beyond the Dneiper River, beyond the great city of Kiev almost to the River Donets—was slowly swallowed up by the Russian Empire as Russia waged, and won, wars and territory from this neighbor over several centuries.

After a series of diplomatic and military conflicts between Russia and Poland, the Eternal Peace Treaty of 1686 allowed the Russian Tsar to take authority over Riga, Kiev and the cities of Smolensk and

Poltava. These were cities formerly under Polish-Lithuanian rule. The Russian Empire was expanding westward.

It took another century and the ambitions of Catherine the Great during her reign (1762-1796) for Russia to expand its empire yet further westward so as in effect to swallow up two thirds of the former Polish-Lithuanian state (at the time commonly called Kingdom of Poland). Catherine's successes in diplomatic and military efforts were followed by succeeding Tsars, who after the defeat of Napoleon in 1814 and the Congress of Vienna in 1815, acquired what was left of the great Polish-Lithuanian Confederation. In another big gulp, Poland as an independent nation disappeared, finally becoming a state under the Russian Empire.

The Pale of Settlement was the Tsarist answer to the question of what to do with more than a million Jewish people whose homelands the Empire had acquired in the late 18th and the early 19th centuries. Empress Catherine created the Pale to "control" the Jewish populations living in her newly acquired lands.

This is the backdrop for the formation of the Russian Pale of Settlement. These newly acquired lands were inhabited by many diverse ethnic groups including Jews because the Polish-Lithuanian

197

Union when it had existed had established, even in its foundational documents, a legal doctrine of religious tolerance. Russia under the Tsars, on the contrary, had little exposure to Jews and no basis whatsoever (legal or secular) for religious tolerance. Russia was a singularly Orthodox state with neither experience, understanding, nor tolerance of Jews or any non-believers. Yet Jews were now subjects of Catherine. Ad hoc management (and resulting confusion) entailed. Jews were treated separately. Separate tax rates, for sure. But in keeping with the tradition of Russian rulers in general, the most significant limiting factor was the requirement for special permissions—for where a Jew might reside, as well as for what economic activity he/she could engage in.

Special permissions were not new to the Tsarist way of governing, but the Jewish people were new to the Tsars. Catherine, and the Tsars who followed her, each with their varying degree of intolerance and anti-Semitism, put their own particular cast of color to the setting of controls. A common tradition under Russian rule in general—*everything is prohibited unless it is especially permitted*—permeated life for the Jews. Under Catherine these permissions for her new Jewish subjects were still inchoate, ambiguous, contradictory and often relied on lower level officials to implement (at their whim). Tsars who came after Catherine toughened these matters with clearer and stricter controls over where Jews could reside and in what economic activities they could engage.

The Pale's various evolving forms after Catherine, and the intricacies of what was and was not allowed by the Tsars who followed her, are interesting historically but for us right now what's important is that Eli—leaving Russia for America—was hopping the fence so to speak, leaving that restrictive life, and hoping the same, soon, I assume, for his wife and children.

...nformation can be obtained
...CGtesting.com
...the USA
...33070420
...00001B/1

9 781644 692806